Books by Efraín Huerta

ABSOLUTO AMOR (1935)

LINEA DEL ALBA (1936)

POEMAS DE GUERRA Y ESPERANZA (1943)

LOS HOMBRES DEL ALBA (1944)

LA ROSA PRIMITIVA (1950)

LOS POEMAS DEL VIAJE (1953)

ESTRELLA EN ALTO (1956)

EL TAJÍN (1963)

RESPONSOS (1968)

POESIA, 1935-1968 (Selected Poems) (1968)

POEMAS PROHIBIDOS Y DE AMOR (1973)

LOS EROTICOS Y OTRAS POEMAS (1974)

CIRCUITO INTERIOR (1977)

TRANSA-POETICA (1980)

ESTAMPIDA DE POEMINIMOS (1980)

POESIA COMPLETA (Collected Poems) (1988)

500,000
AZALEAS

The Selected Poems of
Efraín Huerta

Translated by Jim Normington
Edited by Jack Hirschman
Introduction by Ilan Stavans

CURBSTONE PRESS

FIRST EDITION, 2001
Copyright © 2001 by Andrea M. Huerta
Translation copyright © 2001 by Jim Normington
All Rights Reserved

Printed on acid free paper by Transcontinental Book Group
Cover design and illustration by Les Kanturek

This book was published with the support of Fideicomiso para la Cultura
México-EUA (U.S.–Mexico Fund for Culture), The Connecticut Commission
on the Arts, The National Endowment for the Arts, and contributions from
many individuals.

The poems which are contained in this edition in English translation were
selected from the Spanish originals in the book *Efraín Huerta, POESIA
COMPLETA*, published in 1988 by Fondo de Cultura Economica in Mexico
City. All Spanish originals are © by the heirs of Efraín Huerta.

Library of Congress Cataloging-in-Publication Data

  Huerta, Efraín.
    500,000 azaleas : the selected poems of Efraín Huerta / translated
    by Jim Normington; edited by Jack Hirschman; introduction by Ilan
    Stavans —— 1st ed.
        p. cm.
    ISBN 1-880684-73-X
      I. Title: Five hundred thousand azaleas. II. Normington, Jim.
    III. Hirschman, Jack,1933- IV. Title.

PQ7297.H84 A6 2000
861'.62—dc21   041366

Printed in Canada
published by
  CURBSTONE PRESS   321 Jackson Street   Willimantic, CT 06266
        e-mail: info@curbstone.org   www.curbstone.org

ACKNOWLEDGMENTS

With special thanks to Dennis Lawson, for his hard work and dedication in preparing the manuscript for production. And special thanks to Jane Blanshard, Matthew and Maria Proser, Barbara Rosen and Roger Wolfe for many helpful comments.

CONTENTS

FOREWORD

by Ilan Stavans

Efraín Huerta's friends nicknamed him "the crocodile," a fitting title, no doubt, for the reptile is known, in folklore at least, for its thick, armor-like skin and for long, tapering jaws and combative demeanor, but it is also docile and susceptible. The image fits Huerta to the finger: he is best known for a type of lyrical poetry almost extinct today devoted to explorations of love and solitude; he fuses eroticism with a fight against injustice; throughout his sixty-eight years, he nurtured a deep-seated faith in human redemption, which took him from an initial infatuation with Marxism to an interest in street voices delivered without conde-scension. But what is most intriguing is that at first sight Huerta's oeuvre seems menacing and even cold, yet at a closer look it reveals itself to be the product of a subtle heart. "Llora lágrimas de cocodrilo," the popular Mexican song says—he cries a crocodile's tears. In English the metapahor suggests a lack of integrity, yet Huerta values conviction and honesty above all.

He belongs to a generation of Mexican poets born at the time of World War I (his birth year is 1914) that gathered around the magazine *Taller*, which published a total of twelve issues between 1938 and 1941 and included, among other contributors, Octavio Paz, Rafael Solana, Enrique González Martínez, Alberto Quintero Álvarez and Neftalí Beltrán. It was a deluxe periodical that served as a model of esthetic commitment. The late thirties were a decade of intense political turmoil and Huerta was a leading figure in the group, the one that remained most loyal to his pro-Soviet affiliation. That affiliation, in fact, from his glorification of Joseph Stalin as a redeemer of sorts in his book *Poemas de guerra y esperanza* (1943) to his praise of the U.S.S.R. in his poem "Des-cubrimiento de Moscú," included in *Los poemas de viaje* (1945), is a low point in his artistic quest—not unique in a continent whose artists have at times been blinded by the oratory of a fascist state masked as messianic. But Huerta is not a poet easy to pigeonhole.

He matured, using his talents not only to shock but to narrate his outer and inner life and his engagement with a landscape—that of Mexico City at an age of colossal growth that often turns the artist into a casualty. Huerta's thick skin combined with his daring *joie de vivre* makes him a fascinating poet, a kind of compass useful to signal the contradictions of a modernity haphazardly implemented south of the Rio Grande.

Octavio Paz included a handful of Huerta's poems in *New Poetry of Mexico*, a volume published by E. P. Dutton in 1970. (The volume was edited by Mark Strand.) To my knowledge, that was the first and only time Huerta appeared in English before this anthology, patiently translated by Jim Normington and edited by Jack Hirschman. In it Huerta's entire gamut of personal influences, as well as his pantheon of heroes, are all in display. He began as a Surrealist infatuated by Paul Eluard, then moved on in reaction to the ideological ambiguity of the generation of poets prior to his, known as *Los Contemporáneos*, to an affiliation to the Communist Party, as a result of which he befriended the novelist José Revueltas. *500,000 Azaleas* contains tributes to Roque Dalton, "Che" Guevara, and Federico García Lorca at the time of their deaths, as well as hidden homages to Pablo Neruda and poems dedicated to as disparate figures as Paz and the Cuban poet and essayist Roberto Fernández Retamar.

Mexico for Huerta is a source of constant ambivalence. The extent of his engagement with its past and present is manifold. At one point he intones a celebration to President Lázaro Cárdenas' nationalization of the oil industry in 1938, while elsewhere, he invokes a "liberty with its face of a dog" and sings to muralists Diego Rivera and José Clemente Orozco as symbols of resistance. He attacks the Catholic Church as built on dishonesty and intrigue and accuses it of betraying its people. This passion is best exemplified in lines from "My Country, Oh My Country!":

> Loving, yearning, miserable, opulent,
> Country that doesn't answer, country of sorrow.
> A child who questions seems like a dead child.

The zeitgeist was fertile for Huerta as poet to indulge in political debates, a quality altogether absent from the esthetics of today's generation. In this poem he looks at U.S.-Mexican relations with suspicion. He ridicules Washington's foreign loans, with its numerous tentacles.

> Thank you, Golden Calf! Thank you, FBI!
> Thank you, a thousand thanks, dear Mister President!
> Thank you, honorable bankers, honest industrialists,
> generous monopolists, sweet speculators;
> thank you, industrious estate owners,
> thank you a thousand times, glorious country-sellers,
> thank you, people of order.

In "El Tajín" he—as do many other contributors to *Taller*, especially Paz—approaches the pre-Columbian ruins as a loci to reflect on the treacherous twists of history. (It serves as a suitable counterpoint to Paz's "Himno entre ruinas").

Huerta's oratory is at times hard to take. But his is not a poetry of propaganda that should be forgotten. Quite the contrary—through his work it is possible to revisit, sometimes better than in that of any other poet, the ups and downs of poetry in the Southern hemisphere in the twentieth century. Huerta traveled to the United States, and he chronicled segregation in the South and rightly pointed the finger not only at the Ku Klux Klan but also at an institutionalized racism put upside-down by the Civil Rights era. His poem "Alabama in Bloom," dedicated to Paul Robeson, is quite uncommon in Mexican letters, as is "Mississippi Nocturne." In fact, I cannot think of a poet, let alone an essayist, for whom the fate of Blacks in America is so deeply felt. It is of course present in Cuba's Nicolás Guillén and Chile's Pablo Neruda. But Mexican poetry of that period—actually, from the fifties to the nineties—is overwhelmed by the presence of Paz, and after Fidel Castro's revolution in Cuba, Paz began to slowly oscillate to the center-right, denouncing Neruda and distancing himself from any form of active support of left-wing causes. So luminous is his voice, it easily eclipsed that of many contemporaries, including Huerta. So the reading of such poetry, even if simplistic, feels refreshing today and places Paz's persona in its proper context. Huerta sympathized with Cuba, and his sympathy didn't diminish with time. (Among the island's intellectuals he befriended, and held a standing correspondence, was José Lezama Lima, and it was left to Huerta's son David, author of *Incurable* (1987), to edit an anthology in Mexico of Lezama Lima's work). He empathized with victims worldwide, especially in the U.S., where he felt close to Blacks, as is evident in his tribute to Martin Luther King, Jr., written at the time of his assassination. In it the entire Vietnam era is brought to light in all its strident power. Huerta establishes a bridge between King's tragic death and that of Abraham Lincoln more than a century earlier. He writes:

> When Abraham Lincoln was assassinated
> a bit of dusk fell upon the Black world
> and one after another the prayers followed
> like a bitter river of tears.

When still young Huerta went to law school but switched to journalism in 1936 and contributed to Mexico's leading newspapers. He also worked for quite some time as a film critic. I have with me an album of photographs of his. In one he is next to Mario Moreno "Cantinflas," and in others he stands next to María Félix, Julio Bracho and Emilio "El Indio" Fernández. His work as a reviewer, notwithstanding, hardly ever impedes upon his poetry, perhaps because poetry, Huerta trusts us to know, is anything but entertainment. Its value is in its effort to conceptualize a view of the universe that calls attention to the eros and pathos that inhabit us. He used Hemingway and Kafka as extreme characters to expound on the clash between inspiration and force, between courage and contemplation: the former he saw as a force of nature, made of the "old blood of a bull" but "blessed be that damned blood of yours," whereas the author of *Metamorphosis* was beset to the point that he wrote on his skin the word "abyss." Between these extremes Huerta oscillated.

These and others, for his heart was torn apart between engagement and aloofness. Toward the end of his life—he died in 1982—Huerta practiced a shorter form of poetry, a sort of sarcastic haiku he called poemínimos. (A handful of them, such as "Tame Hyperbole," are included in this anthology.) His best legacy, notwithstanding, is neither those mini-poems, nor his quest for liberty in life and in art, which at times came across in inflammatory fashion. Instead, it is, to my mind, in his songs to Mexico City and in his romantic verses. *500,000 Azaleas* includes examples of both. Their status in Huerta's canon is best appreciated not in isolation but in the flux of his overall poetic vision. "Declaration of Hatred," for instance, is an astonishing portrait of the megalopolis as an angry, all-devouring place. From the first line on, the poet doesn't hesitate to call attention to its bestial qualities. History and the speed of the present collide in it. A city "of ash and volcanic stone," Huerta calls it, a "city of pavement, blood and lifeless sweat," "black," "angry," and "boring"—tepid, nightmarish, a dance of millions of people swallowed by indifference and anonymity. These adjectives echo the invocations of Mexico's colonial poets, like Bernardo de Balbuena, Francisco de Terrazas, and particularly Carlos de Sigüenza y Góngora, and, more recently, in the novels of Carlos Fuentes and José Agustín and the poetry of José Emilio Pacheco, among others. Among them Huerta's stands out as an angry, vociferous viewpoint with a Whitmanesque cadence to it.

Indeed, Huerta strikes me as a poet heavily indebted to *Leaves of Grass*. Many of his urban poems invoke the body electric of Whitman with astonishing power, a Whitman channeled through the eyes and ears of García Lorca. (Neruda once described Huerta as "Mexico's García Lorca.") A poem to the traffic-intense Avenida Juárez, reminiscent of "My Country, Oh My Country!," includes the following stanza:

There's a river of crystals and flames in the air,
A sea of blooming voices, a moan of savagery,
Things and thoughts that wound;
There's the brief murmur of the dawn
And the scream of agony of one night, then another
    night,
All the nights of the world
In the twitching smell of the bitter mouths.

Whitman of course was not about American progress and nationalism, as people tend to think today, but a poet about "the incomparable things," as Emerson suggested, about philosophical and religious principles—in short, about ecstasy. Nothing of the sort might be said of Huerta. Instead, he is very much a political animal: his vision of the urban landscape is fatalistic, of millions of people forming a river of anonymity and indifference. No mysticism in Huerta, no superior force, only an implacable feeling of fatalism for a nation oblivious to its own riches. "How many millions of men will speak English?," he asks. And then says: "One asks the question and one moves away from the same question as if from a burning nail."

Huerta's romantic self is equally assertive but far less thespian and less utopian too. (The scholar Frank Dauster described it as "the sword of eros.") In fact, in it the object of love, represented by women, is a metaphor of the city as a whole. He simultaneously invokes love and hatred when singing to his beloved muse, just as he has a love-hate relationship with Mexico City. Still, tenderness and compassion are qualities of this portion of his oeuvre. "The Clamor of Dawn" is an example. In it he uses romantic elements (flowers, a kiss, a child's sight) to intone feelings of belonging but also confusion. He does the same in "Elegy for a White Rose" and "Dawn from a Star." The latter begins:

From a sky a nard,
from the red solitude,
from my slow, lonely life

I contemplate you existing,
a lengthy kiss, feverish hands,
hair like underwater light.
From a star my perfect desire
And cool customary dawn and hope.

It almost seems impossible that the same poet who sings against colonialism, who pays homage to the leaders of the Civil Rights era, who portrays Mexico's capital as a place that "ought to be and isn't," who portrays "Ché" Guevara's demise as "loaded with the death of centuries," should be capable of such gentle, unideological tonalities. Therein, I'm convinced, Huerta's most compelling characteristic: he is capable of a wide gamut of divergent feelings. "Love is the mercy we possess," he announces. Instead of repressing his vulnerable emotional side, instead of opposing it to the poet engagé that Neruda best personified for him, he allows himself not only to be inhabited by the uncertainty about the durability of human affection but extracts as much juice from such an uncertainty as is possible.

Lágrimas de cocodrilo... Efraín Huerta's poetry is about facades, about the peeling off of layers, about outspokenness and introversion, not as rivals but as complements. He is only ambivalent about the most intimate of feelings but never about politics, a terrain in which he sees no room for doubt. That ambivalence makes him reach levels of astonishing desolation in his work. I know of few artists capable of such extremes.

500,000 Azaleas

ÓRDENES DE AMOR

¡Ten piedad de nuestro amor
y cuídalo, oh Vida!

Carlos Pellicer

1

Amor mío, embellécete.
Perfecto, bajo el cielo, lámpara
de mil sueños, ilumíname.
Orquídea de mil nubes,
desnúdate, vuelve a tu origen,
agua de mis vigilias,
lluvia mía, amor mío.
Hermoso seas por siempre
en el eterno sueño
de nuestro cielo,
amor.

2

Amor mío, ampárame.
Una piedad sin sombra
de piedad es la vida. Sombra
de mi deseo, rosa de fuego.
Voy a tu lado, amor,
como un desconocido.
Y tú me das la dicha
y tú me das el pan,
la claridad del alba
y el frutal alimento,
dulce amor.

LOVE COMMANDS

Have pity on our love
and care for it, oh Life!
Carlos Pellicer

1

Adorn yourself, my love.
Perfect, beneath the sky, lamp
of a thousand dreams, shine on me.
Orchid of a thousand clouds,
undress yourself, return to your beginnings,
water of my fastings,
my rain, my love.
You're beautiful forever
in the everlasting dream
of our sky,
love.

2

Protect me, my love.
Life is a pity without the shadow
of pity. Shadow
of my desire, a rose of fire.
I go along at your side, love,
like a stranger.
And you give me happiness
and you give me bread,
the brightness of dawn
and fruitful nourishment,
sweet love.

3

Amor mío, obedéceme:
ven despacio, así, lento,
sereno y persuasivo:
Sé dueño de mi alma,
cuando en todo momento
mi alma vive en tu piel.
Vive despacio, amor,
y déjame beber,
muerto de ansia,
dolorido y ardiente,
el dulce vino, el vino
de tu joven imperio,
dueño mío.

4

Amor mío, justifícame,
lléname de razón y de dolor.
Río de nardos, lléname
con tus aguas: ardor de ola,
mátame...
     Amor mío.
Ahora sí, bendíceme
con tus dedos ligeros,
con tus labios de ala,
con tus ojos de aire,
con tu cuerpo invisible,
oh tú, dulce recinto
de cristal y de espuma,
verso mío tembloroso,
amor definitivo.

3

Obey me, my love:
come gently, slowly as such,
serene and persuasively:
I know my soul's owner
since every moment
my soul lives inside your skin.
You live gently, love,
and let me, dead of longing,
in pain and burning,
drink the sweet wine, the wine
of your youthful rule,
my master.

4

Justify me, my love,
fill me with reason and grief.
River of nards, fill me
with your waters: heat of the waves,
kill me...
                My love.
Bless me now, yes,
with your thin fingers,
with your winging lips,
with your eyes of airs,
with your invisible body,
oh you sweet enclosure
of crystal and foam,
my trembling poem,
definitive love.

5

Amor mío, encuéntrame.
Aislado estoy, sediento
de tu virgen presencia,
de tus dientes de hielo.
Hállame, dócil fiera,
bajo la breve sombra de tu pecho,
y mírame morir,
contémplame desnudo
acechando tu danza,
el vuelo de tu pie,
y vuélveme a decir
las sílabas antiguas del alba:
Amor, amor-ternura,
amor-infierno,
desesperado amor.

6

Amor, despiértame
a la hora bendita, alucinada,
en que un hombre solloza
víctima de sí mismo y ábreme
las puertas de la vida.
Yo entraré silencioso
hasta tu corazón, manzana de oro,
en busca de la paz
para mi duelo. Entonces
amor mío, joven mía,
en ráfagas la dicha placentera
será nuestro universo.
Despiértame y espérame,
amoroso amor mío.

5

Meet me, my love.
I'm isolated, thirsty
for your virgin presence,
your icy teeth.
Find me, gentle wild one,
under the brief shadow of your chest,
and watch me dying,
think about me naked
eyeing your dance,
the flight of your feet,
and turn to me speaking
the ancient syllables of dawn:
Love, love-tenderness,
love-hellishness,
hopeless love.

6

Love, wake me
at the blessed deluded hour
when a man sobs,
a victim of himself, and open
the doors of life for me.
I'll enter quietly,
right to your heart, a golden apple,
in search of peace
for my sorrow.
Then my love, my young one,
happiness in pleasing flashes
will be our universe.
Wake me and expect me,
my loving love.

TERNURA

Lo que más breve sea:
la paloma, la flor,
la luna en las pupilas;
lo que tenga la nota más suave:
el ala con la rosa,
los ojos de la estrella;
lo tierno, lo sencillo,
lo que al mirarse tiembla,
lo que se toca y salva
como salvan los ángeles,
como salva el verano
a las almas impuras;
lo que nos da ventura e igualdad
y hace que nuestra vida
tenga el mismo sabor
del cielo y la montaña.
Eso que si besa purifica.
Eso, amiga: tus manos.

TENDERNESS

That which is briefest:
the dove, the flower,
the moon in the eyes;
that which has the smoothest note:
the wing with the rose,
the eyes of a star;
what's tender, what's simple,
what sees itself trembling,
what touches and saves
as angels save,
as summer saves
impure souls;
that which gives us bliss and equality
and makes our life
have the same taste
for sky and mountain.
That which if kissed is cleansed.
That is, sweetheart: your hands.

LA AUSENTE

Arriba del silencio,
con la luz en declive,
mi retrato de niebla.
Puramente un clavel
y una gladiola. Y tú,
dominadora de ti misma,
aguja en mi cerebro,
síntesis de me edad.
La meditación diaria,
como una resbaladiza
palabra de ternura,
se me clava en el pecho:
seguramente oye
la rapidez absurda de mi sangre
o el fin de tu recuerdo
sobre mi piel. Arriba,
donde las palabras se vuelven
pedazos de cielo, un algo
de mi muerte se siente.
Tiniebla tibia, dibujo
de mi voz.

THE MISSING ONE

Upwards of the silence,
with the light slanting down,
my misty likeness.
Merely a carnation
and a gladiola. And you,
dominatrix of yourself,
needle in my mind,
synthesis of my age.
The daily meditation,
like slippery
words of tenderness,
jabs me in the chest:
surely it listens to
the absurd urgency of my blood
or the end of your memory
on my skin. Overhead,
where words turn into
pieces of sky, I sense
a fragment of my demise.
Warm darkness, image
of my voice.

LA RAÍZ AMARGA

Ahora viene la raíz amarga, el ansioso,
negruzco paso; viene también
la tiniebla de llanto, la dorada,
ciega y amante miseria. Ya se acerca,
tigre y mutilación, la desgarrada voz.

Ahora no viene nadie.
Ni un héroe en desamparo
ni una mujer ni un niño.
Ni una pasión ni una palabra.
Duele el silencio. La piel se muere de silencio.
¿Dónde está esa maldita piedad? Oh llamarada.
Buscadla entre una y otra soledad.

Ahora venid a verlo, sacado de raíz,
muerto un millón de veces, tirado ahí,
pirámide bandera incertidumbre
doliéndose
endurecido cicatrizado
país patria nación
territorio ardientemente amado.

¿Quién habla, quién nos llama desde el frío,
desde aquella sorda celda, desde nuestros muertos?
¿Acaso no estamos en un lecho de rosas?
Quémate, árdete, púdrete los pies los ojos
oh libertad oh justicia,
niñas de dulce voz de hambre
pequeñas niñas de metal dolorido.
                No viene nadie.

THE BITTER ROOT

Now the bitter root comes, the anxious
blackish footstep; the darkness of weeping
comes too, the golden, blind, loving
misery. Now it comes closer,
the torn voice, jaguar and mutilation.

Now nobody comes.
Neither a helpless hero,
nor a woman or a child.
Not passion or a single word.
The silence pains. Skin dies of it.
Where is that damned mercy? Oh flame!
Look for it between one and another solitude.

Now come see it, entirely removed,
dead a million times, thrown down over there,
a pyramid flag of uncertainty
hurting itself
a hardened scarred
country homeland nation
territory passionately loved.

Who's speaking, who's calling to us from the cold,
from that deaf cell, from our dead?
Maybe it's not a bed of roses we're in?
Burn, burn and rot, your feet and eyes
oh liberty oh justice,
little girls with sweet hungry voices,
tiny little girls with a metal-like grieving.
          Nobody's coming.

Desde el miedo, desde el pavor, entonces,
hay que hablar, decir las cosas por su secreto nombre,
por el nombre y en nombre del poeta y del artista,
por los encendidos, los dueños de la calle,
dueños del amor ay amor ay dolencia
ay cárcel mía, cárcel de todos.
Si tenéis la patria por cárcel no tenéis nada.
Si respiráis libertad respiráis muerte
la tibia y democrática muerte
el juego de la muerte
muerte calavera de azúcar
alianza para el progreso de la muerte.

La libertad con su cara de perro
cara de policía
danza una negra danza
(soy libre para decir como esclavo lo que me da la gana)
desde el mármol de Juárez, tan libre,
hasta la libertad de Lecumberri.

Mordamos la raíz amarga,
duro cristal, seca raíz del alba,
amorosa y angélica raíz.
        ¿Es que no viene nadie?
Vamos a verlo, entonces,
con sus ojos de roja fiebre y sus heridas de sal.
Vamos a verlo: un lápiz, un pincel, su enfermedad.
Ya vienen todos.
Rios vienen van cordilleras ruinas
celebraciones centenarias aturden.
Diego ha muerto. José Clemente ha muerto.
David vive. David ama.
Hablémosle en voz baja. Ya vamos.
Démosle una estela un dios de barro
un laurel un apretón de manos plata de Guanajuato,

14

After the fear, after the terror, then,
one must speak, must say things for its secret name,
for the name and in the name of the poet and the artist,
the fiery ones, the masters of the street,
masters of love oh love oh disease
oh prison of mine, prison of everyone.
If you have a country as a prison you have nothing.
If you breathe liberty you're breathing death;
tepid and democratic death,
the game of death,
sugar skull death,
an alliance with the progress of death.

Liberty with its face of a dog,
its policeman's face,
dances a dark dance
(and I'm free to speak as a slave who's paid his dues)
from the marble of Juarez, so very free,
all the way to the liberty of Lecumberri.

We bite the bitter root,
the hard crystal, the dry root of the dawn,
the tender angelical root.
          Is this why nobody comes?
Let's go look at it then,
with its feverish eyes and its salty wounds.
Let's go look at it: a pencil, a paintbrush, their disease.
Now everything comes.
Rivers come running, mountain ranges, ruins,
centennial celebrations are stunned.
Diego Rivera is dead. Jose Clemente is dead.
David lives. David loves.
Let's speak to him in a low voice. Now let's go.
Let's make him a path, a god of mud,
a laurel, a silver handshake from Guanajuato,

démosle un corazón de jade un saludo de Pablo Neruda
palomas mil palomas
el cadáver de un juez
un poema de Paul Eluard
un cielo virginal
una tempestad
para que viva
que viva
rodeado de amorosas raíces
de verdadera libertad.

let's give him a jade heart,
a greeting from Pablo Neruda,
doves, a thousand doves
the corpse of a judge
a poem of Paul Eluard
a virginal sky
a storm
so that he lives
         lives
surrounded by loving roots
         by authentic liberty.

LA MUCHACHA EBRIA

Este lánguido caer en brazos de una desconocida,
esta brutal tarea de pisotear mariposas y sombras y cadáveres;
este pensarse árbol, botella o chorro de alcohol,
huella de pie dormido, navaja verde o negra;
este instante durísimo en que una muchacha grita,
gesticula y sueña por una virtud que nunca fue la suya.
Todo esto no es sino la noche,
sino la noche grávida de sangre y leche,
de niños que se asfixian,
de mujeres carbonizadas
y varones morenos de soledad
y misterioso, sofocante desgaste.
Sino la noche de la muchacha ebria
cuyos gritos de rabia y melancolía
me hirieron como el llanto purísimo,
como las náuseas y el rencor,
como el abandono y la voz de las mendigas.

Lo triste es este llanto, amigos, hecho de vidrio molido
y fúnebres gardenias despedazadas en el umbral de
las cantinas,
llanto y sudor molidos, en que hombres desnudos, con
sólo negra barba
y feas manos de miel se bañan sin angustia, sin tristeza:
llanto ebrio, lágrimas de claveles, de tabernas enmohecidas,
de la muchacha que se embriaga sin tedio ni pesadumbre,
de la muchacha que una noche—y era una santa noche—
me entregara su corazón derretido,
sus manos de agua caliente, césped, seda,
sus pensamientos tan parecidos a pájaros muertos,
sus torpes arrebatos de ternura,
su boca que sabía a taza mordida por dientes de borrachos,
su pecho suave como una mejilla con fiebre,

THE DRUNKEN GIRL

This languid collapsing into the arms of an unknown girl,
this brutal job of trampling butterflies, shadows, corpses:
this idea of yourself as a tree, a bottle, a stream of alcohol,
a print of a sleeping foot, a green or black jackknife;
this harshest of moments when a girl screams,
winces and dreams of morals she never had.
All this is not only night,
but night pregnant with blood and milk,
with suffocating children,
with women burned to carbon
and men swarthy with loneliness
and mysterious deadly wear and tear.
It's the night of the drunken girl
whose sad angry screams
wounded me like purest weeping,
like a sickness or an old grudge,
like abandonment and the voices of begging girls.

These are sad tears, friends, made of worn-down glass
and dried gardenias shredded to bits in the doorways of bars,
a worn-out weeping and sweat in which men, naked except for
    black beards
and ugly honey-colored hands, wash themselves without
    anguish or sadness;
a drunken weeping, tears for carnations, for mildewed taverns,
for the girl neither bored nor unhappy but who gets drunk,
for the girl who one night, one sacred night,
gave me her melting heart,
her hands of hot water, of young grasses and silk,
her thoughts so similar to dying birds,
her brief flashes of tenderness,
her mouth tasting like a cup gnawed by drunken teeth,
her breasts soft as a fevered cheek,

y sus brazos y piernas con tatuajes,
y su naciente tuberculosis,
y su dormido sexo de orquídea martirizada.

Ah la muchacha ebria, la muchacha del sonreír estúpido
y la generosidad en la punta de los dedos,
la muchacha de la confiada, inefable ternura para un hombre,
como yo, escapado apenas de la violencia amorosa.
Este tierno recuerdo siempre será una lámpara frente
    a mis ojos,
una fecha sangrienta y abatida.

¡Por la muchacha ebria, amigos míos!

her tattooed arms and legs,
her incipient tuberculosis
and her sleeping cunt like a martyred orchid.

Ah the drunken girl, the girl with the silly smile
and freedom at her fingertips,
the girl with that trusting unspeakable sweetness for a man,
a man like me, barely escaped from loving violence.
This tender memory will always be a lamp before my eyes,
a bloody and humbling date.

My friends, here's to the drunken girl!

¡MI PAÍS, OH MI PAÍS!

Ardiente, amado, hambriento, desolado,
bello como la dura, la sagrada blasfemia;
país de oro y limosna, país y paraíso,
país-infierno, país de policías.
Largo río de llanto, ancha mar dolorosa,
república de ángeles, patria perdida.
País mío, nuestro, de todos y de nadie.
Adoro tu miseria de templo demolido
y la montaña de silencio que te mata.
Veo correr noches, morir los días, agonizar las tardes.
Morirse todo de terror y de angustia.
Porque ha vuelto a correr la sangre de los buenos
y las cárceles y las prisiones militares son para ellos.
Porque la sombra de los malignos es espesa y amarga
y hay miedo en los ojos y nadie habla
y nadie escribe y nadie quiere saber nada de nada,
porque el plomo de la mentira cae, hirviendo,
sobre el cuerpo del pueblo perseguido.
Porque hay engaño y miseria
y el territorio es un áspero edén de muerte cuartelaria.
Porque al granadero lo visten
de azul de funeraria y lo arrojan
lleno de asco y alcohol
contra el maestro, el petrolero, el ferroviario,
y así mutilan la esperanza
y le cortan el corazón y la palabra al hombre—
y la voz oficial, agria de hipocresía,
proclama que primero es el *orden*
y la sucia consigna la repiten
los micos de la Prensa,
los perros voz-de-su-amo de la televisión,
el asno en su curul,

MY COUNTRY, OH MY COUNTRY!

Passionate, beloved, starving, desolate,
beautiful as the harsh yet sacred blasphemy;
country of gold and charity, country and paradise,
hell-country, country of cops.
Long river of tears, wide painful sea,
republic of angels, lost native land.
My country, ours, for everyone and for nobody.
I adore your demolished temple misery
and the mountain of silence which kills you.
I see nights running, days dying, afternoons agonizing.
Everything dying of terror and anguish.
Because the blood of the good ones is running again
and the jails and the military prisons are for them.
Because the shadow of the malignant ones is dense
and bitter and there's fear in their eyes and nobody
speaks and nobody writes and nobody wants to know
anything about anything, because the lead weight
of the boiling lie falls upon the body
of the persecuted nation.
Because there's fraud and misery
and the territory is a rough paradise of military destruction.
Because the Guard covers it with the blue
of a funeral parlor and they fling it
full of disgust and alcohol against
teacher, saboteur, and railway man,
and so they cripple hope and cut
the heart and the word of mankind;
and the official voice, sour with hypocrisy,
proclaims that first is *order*
and the scoundrels of the press
repeat the filthy slogan,
along with the voice-of-their-masters television dogs,
the ass in his official chair,

el *león* y el rotario,
las secretarias y ujieres del Procurador
y el poeta callado en su muro de adobe,
mientras la dulce patria temblorosa
cae vencida en la calle y en la fábrica.
Éste es el panorama:
Botas, culatas, bayonetas, gases...
¡Viva la libertad!

Buenavista, Nonoalco, Pantaco, Veracruz...
todo el país amortajado, todo,
todo el país envilecido,
todo eso, hermanos míos,
¿no vale mil millones de dólares en préstamo?
¡Gracias, Becerro de Oro! ¡Gracias, FBI!
¡Gracias, mil gracias, *Dear Mister President!*
Gracias, honorables banqueros, honestos industriales,
generosos monopolistas, dulces especuladores;
gracias, laboriosos latifundistas,
mil veces gracias, gloriosos vendepatrias,
gracias, gente de orden.
Demos gracias a todos
y rompamos
con un coro solemne de gracia y gratitud
el silencio espectral que todo lo mancilla.
¡Oh país mexicano, país mío y de nadie!
Pobre país de pobres. Pobre país de ricos.
¡Siempre más y más pobres!
¡Siempre menos, es cierto,
pero siempre más ricos!

Amoroso, anhelado, miserable, opulento,
país que no contesta, país de duelo.
Un niño que interroga parece un niño muerto.
Luego la madre pregunta por su hijo
y la respuesta es un mandato de aprehensión.

the Lion and the Rotary Club member,
the secretaries and doormen of the Representative,
and the poet silent behind his adobe walls
while the sweet trembling native land
falls defeated in the street and in the factory.
This is the scenario:
Boots, rifle butts, bayonets, tear gas...
Long Live liberty!

Buenavista, Nonoalco, Pantaco, Veracruz...
the entire country shrouded, all of it,
the entire country degraded,
—well, my brothers, wasn't all that
worth a thousand million bucks on loan?
Thank you, Golden Calf! Thank you, FBI!
Thank you, a thousand thanks, *Dear Mister President!*
Thank you, honorable bankers, honest industrialists,
generous monopolists, sweet speculators;
thank you, industrious estate owners,
thank you a thousand times, glorious country-sellers,
thank you, people of order.
Let's give thanks to everybody
and with a solemn chorus of grace and gratitude
break the ghostly silence
which stains everything.
Oh country of Mexico, my country and country of nobody!
Poor land of poor people. Poor country of rich ones.
Always more and more poor people!
Always less, that's for sure,
but always more rich ones!

Loving, yearning, miserable, opulent,
country that doesn't answer, country of sorrow.
A child who questions seems like a dead child.
Later the mother asks her child
and the answer is an apprehensive command.

En los periódicos vemos bellas fotografías
de mujeres apaleadas y hombres nacidos en México
que sangran y su sangre
es la sangre de nuestra maldita conciencia
y de nuestra cobardía.
Y no hay respuesta nunca para nadie
porque todo se ha hundido en un dorado mar de dólares
y la patria deja de serlo
y la gente sueña en conjuras y conspiraciones
y la verdad es un sepulcro.
La verdad la detentan los secuestradores,
la verdad es el fantasma podrido de MacCarthy
y la jauría de turbios, torpes y mariguanos inquisidores
de huaraches;
la verdad está en los asquerosos hocicos de los cazadores
de brujas.
¡La grande y pura verdad patria la poseen,
oh país, país mío, los esbirros,
los soldadones, los delatores y los espías!
No, no, no. La verdad no es la dulce espiga
sino el nauseabundo coctel de barras y de estrellas.
La verdad, entonces, es una democracia nazi
en la que todo sufre, suda y se avergüenza.
Porque mañana, hoy mismo,
el padre denunciará al hijo
y el hijo denunciará a su padre y a sus hermanos.
Porque pensar que algo no es cierto
o que un boletín del gobierno
puede ser falso
querrá decir que uno es comunista
y entonces vendrán las botas de la Gestapo criolla,
vendrán los gases, los insultos,
las vejaciones y las calumnias
y todos dejaremos de ser menos que polvo,
mucho menos que aire o que ceniza,
porque todos habremos descendido

In the newspapers we see the beautiful photographs
of beaten-down women and men born in Mexico
who bleed and their blood
is the blood of our damned conscience
and of our cowardice.
And there's never an answer for anybody
because everything has sunken in a golden sea of dollars
and the native land allows it to be
and the people dream of plots and conspiracies
and truth is a tombstone.
The kidnappers illegally detain the truth,
the truth is the rotten phantom of McCarthy
and a restless pack of wild dogs, dishonest dope smoking
    inquisitors in huarache sandals;
the truth is in the awful angry faces of the witch hunters.
They possess the great pure truth of the native land,
oh country, my country, henchmen, military goons,
    informers and spies!
No, no, no. The Truth is not a sweet ear of wheat
but the sickening cocktail of metal bars and the stars.
The truth, then, is a Nazi democracy
in which everything suffers, sweats, and shames itself.
Because tomorrow, same as today,
the father will denounce his kid
and his kid will denounce his father and his brothers.
Because to think that something is not for sure
or that a communiqué from the Governor
can be false
means that one is a Communist
and then they will sell the boots of the Native Gestapo,
they will sell the gases, the insults,
the abuses and the slander
and we'll all be left less than dust,
much less than air or ashes,
because all of us will have descended

al fondo de la nada,
muertos sin ataúd,
soñando el sueño inmenso
de una patria sin crímenes,
y arderemos, impíos y despiadados,
tal vez rodeados de banderas y laureles,
tal vez, lo más seguro,
bajo la negra niebla
de las más negras maldiciones...

to the bottom of nothing,
dead ones without coffins,
dreaming the immense dream
of a native land without crime,
and we will burn, heartless and cruel,
surrounded maybe by flags and laurels,
maybe, but most certainly,
beneath the black fog
of the blackest curses...

ACERCA DE LA MELANCOLÍA

Cuando el ansia, como amarilla sombra,
endurece los párpados, y el día
sin ruido se ha fugado entre las nubes
lentas y oscurecidas,
un abismo se lanza
sobre los cuerpos
y las almas del mundo.

Sombra a sombra la niebla se agiganta
cegando puertas, bocas,
ventanas y cerebros,
desgarrando edificios,
melodías románticas,
violetas, rosas,
sueños y dulzura.

Entonces la melancolía,
la aceitosa melancolía:
humo blanco en las venas,
como ligeros pétalos clavados
en los nervios y músculos.

La melancolía es otra piel de los hombres.
Otros huesos, otras arterias.
Otros pulmones, otro sexo.
Alguna vez los hombres del subsuelo
dirán que la melancolía
es una gran bandera libertaria.

WITH REGARD TO MELANCHOLY

When anguish, like a yellow shadow,
hardens the eyelids, and the quiet
day has fled among the slow
and darkened clouds,
an abyss throws itself
upon the bodies
and the hearts of the world.

Shadow by shadow the fog grows enormous
sealing off doors, mouths,
windows and brains,
ripping through buildings,
love songs,
violets, roses,
dreams and gentleness.

And then melancholy arrives,
oily melancholy:
white smoke in the veins
and sharp thin petals
in the nerves and muscles.

Melancholy is that other skin of men.
Those other bones, other arteries.
Other lungs, other sex.
Sometimes men of the substrate
say that melancholy
is a great liberating flag.

ALABAMA EN FLOR

A Paul Robeson

500,000 azaleas vende este comerciante cada día,
cada hora, cada semana y cada mes. 500,000 azaleas
para las honradas casas de Alabama y de Georgia,
para las suaves y jóvenes mujeres de la Florida,
para la solemne limpieza de las funerarias
y para el gigante hotel de Nueva Orleans.

Azaleas para todos los gustos y para toda hora:
para la hora del amor bendito, para la hora del sueño
y para la hora en que surgen de las tinieblas
—desenfrenados perros de agonía, malditos—
los blancos y negros caballeros de las flagelaciones,
los señores de horca y cuchillo y cruz ardiendo.

Bellas, breves y venenosas azaleas para el Gran Dragón,
dulcísimas azaleas para la hija del Gran Dragón
y para la tierna y abnegada esposa del Gran Dragón.

¡Una lluvia de azaleas para los *Ku Klux Klanes*
que en las noches siniestras azotan a los negros,
y azotan a los blancos, a las mujeres de los blancos
y a las mujeres de los negros, y a sus hijos, negros y blancos!

¡Millones de azaleas para los encapuchados asesinos
que han hecho de las claras noches de Alabama
y de las claras noches de Georgia un pavoroso infierno!

¡500,000 azaleas como 500,000 resecas maldiciones
para los turbios violadores del descanso y del sueño!

ALABAMA IN BLOOM

for Paul Robeson

This merchant sells 500,000 azaleas every day,
every hour, every week, every month. 500,000 azaleas
for the honorable households of Alabama and Georgia,
for the soft young women of Florida,
for the solemn cleanliness of funeral parlors
and for the enormous New Orleans hotel.

Azaleas for everyone's taste and for every hour:
for the hour of blessed love, for the hour of sleep
and for the hour when from the darkness surface
—wild dogs of agony—damned
the white and black knights of flagellations,
the men with pitchforks, knives, and a burning cross.

Beautiful, brief, poisonous azaleas for the Grand Dragon,
sweetest smelling azaleas for the daughter of the Grand Dragon
and for the tender yet cowering wife of the Grand Dragon.

A deluge of azaleas for the Ku Klux Klan
who whip the blacks on sinister evenings
and whip the whites, the women of the whites
and black women, and children both black and white!

Millions of azaleas for the hooded murderers
who have made the clear Alabama nights
and the clear Georgia nights a terrible hell!

500,000 azaleas like 500,000 dry curses
for the unruly violators of sleep and dreams!

¡500,000 azaleas como 500,000 azotes para los *KKK*,
repulsivo hervidero de la Edad Media y sucia podredumbre
en el fatigado corazón de las civilizaciones!

500,000 azaleas like 500,000 lashes from the KKK,
repulsive medieval swarm and filthy corruption
in the worn-out heart of civilizations!

CANCIÓN

La luna tiene su casa
Pero no la tiene
la niña negra
la niña negra de Alabama

La niña negra sonríe
y su sonrisa
brilla como si fuera
la cuchara de plata
de los pobres

La luna tiene su casa
Pero la niña negra no tiene casa
la niña negra
la niña negra de Alabama

SONG

The moon has a house
but the little black girl doesn't
the little black girl in Alabama

The little black girl smiles
and her smile
shines as if it were
the silver spoon
of the poor

The moon has a house
but the little black girl
doesn't have a house
the little black girl
the little black girl in Alabama

LAKE CHARLES, LA.

Para Carlos Mora

El blues salió de los rincones.
El negro seguía sudando a chorros.
Sudaba sangre negra, sudor negro.
Waiting Room Colored...White.
This is the Amazing America.
En realidad, el sur de Norteamérica.
El blues, oh Dixieland,
oh soberanos pelícanos,
seguía corriendo por los rincones.
Noche a noche, un blues se ahoga
en las orillas del Mississippi.

LAKE CHARLES, LOUISIANA

for Carlos Mora

The blues rises up from the corners.
The black man goes on sweating profusely.
Sweating black blood, black sweat.
Waiting Room Colored... White.
This is the Amazing America.
In reality, the south in North America.
The blues, oh Dixieland,
oh sovereign pelicans,
continue running around the corners.
Night after night, a blues is drowning
down by the banks of the Mississippi.

NOCTURNO DEL MISSISSIPPI

En estos precisos momentos todo momento es bello. Por
    ejemplo:
que los jóvenes negros se amen a la orilla del río,
bajo el ruinoso techo del Eads Bridge,
y que su risa sea del color de la carne y de su espesa piel.
Que se amen larga y estrechamente al amparo del cielo,
como se aman todos los que aman,
y que sus besos sean el pequeño prodigio del vuelo en la
    paloma.

Que el río solloce y siga su camino hacia el mar
y los jóvenes negros sean sus propias estatuas.
Que la pequeña negra maldiga de su sombra
y el negro, entonces, la desnude.
Que una paloma muerta quede ahí, hecha cenizas,
y el amor resucite a la orilla del alba.
Que los jóvenes negros sean la negra ternura,
el más amargo y doloroso amor,
y que el llanto del río, llanto de sucios ojos,
prosiga su infinito morir bajo la tibia luna.

MISSISSIPPI NOCTURNE

In these precise moments every moment is beautiful. For
    example:
how the young blacks make love
on the riverbank beneath the broken-down roof of the
    Eads Bridge,
and how their laughter is the color of flesh and their thick skin.
How they make love a long long time
intimately beneath the sheltering sky,
as all who love make love,
and how their kisses are the little prodigy of the flight of a
    dove.

How the river weeps and continues its path toward the sea,
and the young blacks are its fitting statues.
How the little black woman curses her shadow
and the black man then undresses her.
How a dead dove made of ashes remains there
and love returns to life at break of day.
How the young blacks are black tenderness,
the most bitter most sorrowful love,
and how the weeping of the river, a weeping of dirty eyes,
continues its infinite dying beneath the tepid moon.

LA LLUVIA

Cae sobre los millones de cabezas de ganado,
sobre los millones de mercados,
sobre los millones de pequeñas y grandes iglesias,
sobre millones y millones de Biblias.
Sobre los verdes pastos y la mano rugosa del granjero,
sobre las rubias cabelleras y los millones de ojos azules.
Cae sobre San Antonio a la hora del acento de las campanas,
y es como si cayera de los cielos
un poema infinito
o millones de labios de millones de ángeles.
Cae sobre la llanura azul y verde.
Llega siempre "como caída del cielo".
Cae pesadamente sobre la tienda de Cletus Brown
y da de beber al poderoso río.
Cae con una fina conciencia de ser lluvia,
y es como si fuera la primera vez que lloviera en el mundo.
Así se explica uno que cuando llueve en Texas
el hombre redescubra el sentido natural de la tierra.

RAIN

Rain is falling on millions of heads of cattle,
on millions of market places,
on millions of huge and tiny cathedrals,
on millions and millions of Bibles.
It falls on the green pastures and the wrinkled hands of farmers,
on the red-haired ones and on millions of blue eyes.
It falls on San Antonio at the hour when bells begin ringing,
it's as if an endless poem
had fallen from the skies
or millions of lips of millions of angels.
It falls on the green and blue plains.
Every time it happens "it's like the sky has fallen."
It falls heavily on Cletus Brown's store,
and gives a drink to the swollen river.
It falls with a fine awareness of being rain
and as if it were the first time it rained on the world.
When a man explains this rain in Texas
he rediscovers the natural feeling of the earth.

EL CABALLO ROJO

Para Eugenia Huerta

Era un caballo rojo galopando sobre el inmenso rio.
Era un caballo rojo, colorado, colorado
"como la sangre que corre cuando matan un venado".
Era un caballo rojo con las patas manchadas de angustioso
    cobalto.
Agonizó en el río a los pocos minutos. Murió en el rio.
La noche fue su tumba. Tumba de seco mármol
y nubes pisoteadas.

             (St. Louis, Missouri)

THE RED HORSE

for Eugenia Huerta

There was a red horse galloping over the enormous river.
There was a red horse, reddish, reddish,
"like the blood that runs out when they kill a deer."
There was a red horse, its fore-hooves spotted
      with anguished cobalt.
It lay suffering in the river for a few minutes. It died in the river.
The night was its tomb. A tomb of dry marble
and trampled clouds.

(St. Louis, Missouri)

LOS FANTASMAS

Árboles, casas, puentes: los fantasmas.
Era una larga niebla sollozante,
pegada al suelo, espesa, estéril,
monstruosa y agobiante, inmunda forma.

Rostros, piernas y manos: los fantasmas.
Y un frío animal bajo la piel del alma.

Era un mundo de plomo este mundo de Ohio.
Primer alba de plomo y de sucia caricia.

Gemidos, besos, risas: los fantasmas.
Grises, verdes fantasmas del deseo y del miedo.
Era como ir muriendo a la mitad del sueño,
fantasma de mí mismo, fiel derrota.

(West Lafayette, Ohio)

PHANTOMS

Trees, houses, bridges: phantoms.
There's a heavy weeping mist,
stuck to the ground, thick, sterile,
monstrous and exhausting, a filthy mold.

Faces, legs, and hands: phantoms.
And a frigid animal under the skin of the soul.

It's a world of lead, this Ohio world.
Original dawn of lead and dirty petting.

Moans, kisses, laughter: phantoms.
Grey and green phantoms of desire and fear.
It's like a phantom of my very self,
going off to die in the middle of a dream, right on course.

(West Lafayette, Ohio)

HOTEL *EL COLONY*
(Isla de Pinos)

A Roberto Fernández Retamar

Los siniestros *tycoons* con cara de zapato pecoso
lo planearon y construyeron para su alcohólico *week-end*

Costó una escamita de la serpiente *Wall Street*

Habrían de llegar los ventrudos los dispépticos
los ulcerosos los sicópatas los artríticos
y sus bestialmente bellas secretarias

Vendrían los rufianes contratados por George Raft
y la más selecta y vibrante putería de Las Vegas

Ellos bailarían desnudos para imponer el diente sucio de
la chequera
Ellas bailarían desnudas como lombrices de las tuberías

Debieron correr ríos agitados de whisky
y quemarse kilos y kilos de la verdemente liviana mariguana
La ruleta debería girar como la sierpe loca en el abismo
y los dólares suavizar la brutalidad de la resaca

"Venga al Hotel *El Colony*
                    el paraíso de la orgía!"

Pensaban inaugurarlo el primero de enero.

THE COLONY HOTEL
(Pinos Island)

for Roberto Fernández Retamar

The crooked tycoons with freckled, shoe-leather faces
planned and constructed it for their alcoholic weekends

It cost one little scale from the serpent called Wall Street

The potbellied ones the dyspeptics the ulcerous
the psychopaths the arthritics will have arrived
and their beautiful animal-like secretaries

The thugs hired by George Raft will come
and the most select and vibrant whores from Las Vegas

The thugs will dance naked to raise the dirty tooth of prices
The whores will dance naked
like worms in the waterpipes

Excited rivers of whiskey should be flowing
and kilo after kilo of light green marijuana burning
The roulette wheel should be spinning like a crazy snake
and the dollars soothing the savagery of hangovers

"Come to the Colony Hotel,
                            paradise for orgies!"

They're planning to open it January first.

CANTO AL PETRÓLEO MEXICANO

En un crisol de muerte, sepultada,
prisionera marea,
insomnio de la tierra, acumulada,
gigantesca tarea
de los siglos sin fin.
         La desgarrada,
la dulce tierra nuestra
siente cómo gotea
la magistral palpitación siniestra,
la venenosa llama azul,
el poder y la sangre,
la ígnea sangre doliente
de la guerra y el crimen.

No es la plata ni el oro detonante,
sencillos minerales,
no es la leche llameante
de las robustas plantas tropicales,
ni el río poderoso
ni la esbelta cascada
productora de fluido misterioso.

Ni tuvo calidades de moneda
como el cobrizo grano de cacao
en manos de las tribus primitivas.
Es algo más que eso:
es mucho más que todo.

Son extendidas venas abismales,
redes de piedra ardida,
suave manto geológico
cuyas maduras llamas colosales
se alzan en encendida

SONG TO MEXICAN PETROLEUM

Buried in a crucible of death, entombed,
a prisoner tide,
earth's gathered-up insomnia,
the gigantic task
of endless centuries.
                        The torn up
sweet earth of ours
senses how the pompous
throbbing catastrophe,
the poisonous blue flame,
the power and blood,
the igneous sick blood
of war and crime are leaking out.

It's not silver or gold,
those simple minerals, exploding;
it's not milk flaring up
from robust tropical plants,
nor the powerful river
nor the graceful waterfall
producer of mysterious electric.

It doesn't have money-value
like coppery coca seeds
in the hands of primitive tribes.
It's something more than that:
it's much more than everything.

Abysmal veins,
nets of angry stone are stretched,
a smooth geological mantle
whose mature colossal flames
rise up in the fiery shape

figuración de monstruo mitológico,
inmensa bestia herida
por finos instrumentos espectrales.

Nunca el hombre lo viera,
jamás la llama azul nos alumbrara.
Más al indio valiera
quemada sementera
que la ruin ambición; no se compara
el noble campo abierto
con la entraña brutal
por donde bulle incierto
el negro y codiciado mineral.

Y aquella maldición vista en el mundo:
trigales devastados
y hombres asesinados,
es tan sólo un destello del profundo,
del espantoso crimen cometido.
Los antiguos imperios habían sido
un sueño doloroso,
pero sueño,
cuando llegó el petróleo, el escondido
mineral prodigioso,
volvió a nacer el llanto:
y sobre nuestra tierra, en los playones
del viejo Golfo, un canto
de esclavitud se alzó.

Aves de presa con el pico ardiendo
cayeron sobre el suelo
de un México humillado
por la Guerra Civil, y en ese vuelo
venía todo rumor de un desgarrado
sollozar de tragedia.
Largos años de lenta pesadumbre

of a mythological monster,
an enormous beast wounded
by subtle ghostly instruments.

Never had mankind seen it, the blue flame
never had lit the way for us.
But to the Indian
a burning seed bed was worth
more than paltry ambition; you can't compare
the noble open countryside
with the brutal core
where the black coveted mineral
bubbles uncertainly.

And that visible curse in the world—
devastated wheat fields
and assassinated men—
is a spark of wisdom so alone,
of an appalling commitment to crime.
Ancient empires
had been a painful dream
but a dream
when oil arrived, that marvelous
hidden mineral,
weeping got born anew
and over our earth, in the shallows
of the old Gulf, a song
of slavery rose up.

Birds of prey with burning beaks
descended upon the ground
of a Mexico humiliated
by Civil War, and in that flight
every murmur of a shattered
and tragic weeping arrived.
Long years of slow sorrow

siguieron al asalto:
el petróleo corría, la gran riqueza
fabricábase en vano, pues el indio,
de libertades falto,
sólo tenía su pan:
escaso pan de odio y de tristeza.

Años y años pasaron,
el petróleo corría... Sus viejas venas
estallaban en fuego,
el gas iluminaba las serenas
e inquietas selvas.
Años y años pasaron...
Bajo un lóbrego cielo
se efectuaba el pillaje:
cualquiera podía ver cómo crecía
una mancha de sangre en el paisaje.

Pero un buen día, un gran día,
un día que es la bondad del patriotismo,
un día joven como éste, luminoso,
un día genial de gloria,
se oyó un sordo rumor de cataclismo,
de inminente victoria
y jubiloso
resurgir del abismo.
Un alto día como éste
una mano certera señaló
la verdadera ruta de la Patria:
con orgullo que dio
una impresión de fuego sobrehumano,
el michoacano ilustre incorporó
el oro negro al seno mexicano.

followed the assault:
the petroleum ran, great wealth
was built up, in vain, since the Indians,
lacking in liberty,
had only their bread:
a scant bread of hatred and sadness.

Years and years passed,
the petroleum ran... Its aged veins
exploded into fire,
the gas lit up the peaceful
and uneasy jungles.
Years and years passed...
Beneath a dark sky
the plunder was carried out:
anybody could see how bloodstains
had grown on the landscape.

But one good day, one great day,
a day which the goodness of patriotism is,
a day as young and luminous as this,
a day inspired by glory,
the muffled sound of cataclysm,
of imminent victory
and the jubilant
reappearance of the abyss was heard.
One tall day like this
a sure hand pointed out the true path
of the mother country:
with a pride that gave
an impression of a superhuman fire,
the illustrious Michoacan incorporated
the black gold inside the Mexican breast.

En su crisol de muerte, sepultada,
prisionera marea,
la mineral riqueza recobrada
se enciende como tea
iluminando el colosal paisaje.

México es como un árbol
de angustioso follaje:
pero es un árbol libre,
dueño de su destino.

Por eso cuando clama,
cuando la Patria grita toda entera:
"Este es nuestro petróleo,"
la venenosa llama
se funde como cera.
Porque ha llegado el día
y ha llegado la hora
de la grave oración:
es como una
campana de sonora
y vibrante llamada al corazón.

Buried in its crucible of death, entombed,
a prisoner tide,
the recovered mineral wealth
lights up like a torch
illuminating the colossal landscape.

Mexico is like a tree
of anguished leaves:
but it's a free tree,
and master of its destiny.

So that when it cries out,
when the native land shouts as one:
"This is *our* oil"
the poisonous flame
melts like wax.
Because the day has arrived
and the hour has arrived
of a momentous speech:
like a
sounding bell
and a vibrant call to the heart.

ELEGÍA DE LA POLICÍA MONTADA

> Tienen, por eso no lloran,
> de plomo las calaveras.
>
> F. Garcia Lorca

Habría que nombrarlos con una palabra ciega,
porque son mudos como gusanos enloquecidos,
porque tienen manos de plomo, pies y alma de plomo,
porque nombrarlos trae mala suerte y mala muerte.

Decir su nombre de uniforme de canallas, decirlo, maldecirlo,
es como vomitar de miedo
y sentir en la piel un fulgor de agonía.

Un millar de caballos, negros y horribles animales
como ruiseñores cancerosos,
un millar de piedras que no hablan,
dos millares de negras botas,
un millar de sucios relámpagos
que golpean la espalda del pobre.

Negros, negros caballos, negros hombres,
negra y nutrida mariguana para la policía montada.
Toda la triste ciudad se ennegrece de pavor
y la sangre es amarilla
y los niños se pegan a los muros
y las mujeres murmuran que malditos sean.

Los verdaderos hombres nada dicen:
este día siete de noviembre
los hombres se adueñan del alba
y caminan lentamente hacia la Virgen;
llevan rosas y palabras escritas,
palabras poderosas de libertad.

ELEGY FOR THE MOUNTED POLICE

"They have skulls of lead
so they don't weep."
F. Garcia Lorca

I'd have named them with a blind word,
because they're mute like worms gone crazy,
because they have hands of lead, feet and souls of lead,
because to name them brings bad luck and a bad death.

Merely saying their uniformed thug-name, to say it, to curse it,
is like vomiting from fear
and feeling a flash of agony beneath one's skin.

A thousand horses, horrible animals black
like cancerous nightingales,
a thousand stones which do not speak,
two thousand black boots,
a thousand dirty flashes of lightning
who beat upon the backs of the poor.

Black ones; black horses, black men
dark nourishing marijuana for the mounted police.
The entire sad city grows dark with fear
and blood is yellow
and children stick to walls
and the women grumble about how wicked they are.

The honest men don't say anything;
on this day of November seventh
men take control of the dawn
and walk slowly toward the Virgin Mary;
they carry roses and scribbled words,
powerful words about liberty.

Van a ver a la Virgen,
y a cubrirla de flores y de llanto.

Caminan entre un amargo paisaje de sables,
de amargas espinas metálicas,
y la oración es maldición
y ya nunca se sabe cuando los labios dicen
un dulce Ave María
o una dolorida y fecunda mentada de madre.

Porque todo se vuelve turbio
cuando los cuervos a caballo
cabalgan
sombríos
sombras de asesinato
matando todo lo que pisan;
porque los impíos y despiadados llegan
porque son silenciosos
y sólo beben la sangre del crimen
porque nada los detiene
y tienen la piel gruesa de las bestias
porque van a lo suyo y lo suyo es la muerte
y los sables parecen hablar de ruinas
y opacas y melancólicas orgías cuartelarias.

La policía montada no tiene madre.
Es hija del veneno y de la mariguana.
Tienen voz y no hablan.
Pies, pero no caminan.

Feroces y grotescos, sordos y endemoniados,
alcoholizados y apocalípticos,
quiebran la paz del alba
rompen la luz del alma
con sus ojos de lumbre.
Nunca en su vida vieron la llama de una lágrima.

They go to see the Virgin Mary
and to cover her with flowers and tears.

They walk among a bitter landscape of sabers,
among bitter metal thorns,
and the prayer is a curse
and now nobody knows when lips will speak
a sweet Ave Maria
or a sad eloquent celebrated one of the mother.

Because everything turns cloudy
when those crows on horseback
gallop
full of gloom,
dark ones of assassinations
killing everything they trample on;
because the wicked and heartless ones come
because they're silent ones
and drink only the blood of crime,
because nothing stops them
and they have the thick skins of beasts
because they go to what's theirs and what's theirs is death
and the sabers seem to speak of ruins
and of dreamy dim lit orgies in the police barracks.

The mounted police have no mother.
They're the daughter of poison and marijuana.
They have voices but don't speak.
They have feet but don't walk.

Ferocious and grotesque, deaf and demoniacal,
alcoholic and apocalyptic,
they bust up the peace of dawn
they tear up the light of the soul
with their fiery eyes.
Never in their lives have they seen the flame inside a tear.

Cabalgan con la muerte, rumbo a los cementerios,
siempre rumbo a la muerte,
al pie del crimen...

Porque no hay odio para ellos
        malditos sean
porque no hay miedo para ellos
        malditos sean
porque no tienen sangre ni amor
        malditos sean
porque no tienen huesos ni calavera
        malditos sean
porque son negros como una noche de plomo
        malditos sean
porque son sucios y mariguanos
        malditos sean
porque no creen en los ángeles ni en la vida
        malditos sean
porque sólo tienen dientes y sables
        malditos sean
porque son muertos sin sepultura
        malditos sean
porque la palabra se mancha con su nombre
        malditos sean
porque sacrifican la libertad
        ¡malditos sean!

They gallop alongside death in the direction of the graveyards,
always in the direction of death,
at the foot of crime...

Because there's no hatred for them
        goddamn them
because there's no fear for them
        goddamn them
because they don't have blood or love
        goddamn them
because they don't have bones or skulls
        goddamn them
because they're black like a night of gunshots
        goddamn them
because they're filthy marijuana smokers
        goddamn them
because they don't believe in angels or in life
        goddamn them
because they only have teeth and sabers
        goddamn them
because they're dead men without graves
        goddamn them
because the word is stained by their name
        goddamn them
because they slaughter liberty
        goddamn them!

EL TAJÍN

A David Huerta
a Pepe Gelada

... el nombre de El Tajín le fue dado por los
indígenastotonacas de la región por la
frecuencia con que caían rayos sobre
la pirámide...

1

ANDAR así es andar a ciegas,
andar inmóvil en el aire inmóvil,
andar pasos de arena, ardiente césped.
Dar pasos sobre agua, sobre nada
—el agua que no existe, la nada de una astilla—,
dar pasos sobre muertes,
sobre un suelo de cráneos calcinados.

Andar así no es andar sino quedarse
sordo, ser ala fatigada o fruto sin aroma;
porque el andar es lento y apagado,
porque nada está vivo
en esta soledad de tibios ataúdes.
Muertos estamos, muertos
en el instante, en la hora canicular,
cuando el ave es vencida
y una dulce serpiente se desploma.

Ni un aura fugitiva habita este recinto
despiadado. Nadie aquí, nadie en ninguna sombra.
Nada en la seca estela, nada en lo alto.
Todo se ha detenido, ciegamente,
como un fiero puñal de sacrificio.

EL TAJÍN

for David Huerta
and Pepe Gelada

..the name El Tajín was given by the native
Mexican Totonaca Indians of the region
because of the frequency in which sunbeams fell
upon the pyramid...

1

To walk in this direction is to walk blindly,
to walk without motion in motionless air,
to take steps of sand, ardent grass.
To walk on water, on nothing,
—the water which doesn't exist, the nothingness
of a splinter—to walk over the dead,
over ground made of ashen skulls.

To walk this way is not to walk
but to remain deaf, to be an exhausted wing
or a tasteless fruit;
because this walk is slow and lifeless,
because nothing is alive
in this lonely place of tepid coffins.
We're dead, dead
in an instant, in the dog day's hour
when a bird is defeated
and a sweet snake comes crashing down.

Not even a fleeting breeze lives in this merciless place.
Nobody here, nobody in any shadow.
Nothing on the dry trail, nothing up above.
Everything has been held blindly back,
like a fierce sacrificial dagger.

Parece un mar de sangre
petrificada
a la mitad de su ascensión.
Sangre de mil heridas, sangre turbia,
sangre y cenizas en el aire inmóvil.

2

Todo es andar a ciegas, en la
fatiga del silencio, cuando ya nada nace
y nada vive y ya los muertos
dieron vida a sus muertos
y los vivos sepultura a los vivos.
Entonces cae una espada de este cielo metálico
y el paisaje se dora y endurece
o bien se ablanda como la miel
bajo un espeso sol de mariposas.

No hay origen. Sólo los anchos y labrados ojos
y las columnas rotas y las plumas agónicas.
Todo aquí tiene rumores de aire prisionero,
algo de asesinato en el ámbito de todo silencio.
Todo aquí tiene la piel
de los silencios, la húmeda soledad
del tiempo disecado; todo es dolor.
No hay un imperio, no hay un reino.
Tan sólo el caminar sobre su propia sombra,
sobre el cadáver de uno mismo,
al tiempo que el tiempo se suspende
y una orquesta de fuego y aire herido
irrumpe en esta casa de los muertos
—y un ave solitaria y un puñal resucitan.

A sea of petrified blood
appears
in the midst of its cresting.
Blood of a thousand wounds, muddy blood,
blood and ashes in the motionless air.

2

Everything walks blindly in the weary silence
where nothing is born now and nothing is alive
and now the dead have given life
to the dead and the living
bury the living.
And then a sword falls from this metallic sky
and the landscape shines and hardens
or better yet softens like honey
beneath a sun thick with butterflies.

There's no origin. Only the wide carved eyes
and the broken columns and the deathly feathers.
Everything here has a murmuring sound of imprisoned
    air,
a bit of murder within the boundaries of total silence.
Everything here has the skin
of silent ones, the wet solitude
of a preserved time; everything is pain.
There's no empire, there's no king.
Only the traveler over his own shadow,
over the corpse of himself,
in a time when time is suspended
and an orchestra of fire and wounded air
invades this house of the dead—
and a solitary bird and a dagger rise from the dead.

3

Entonces ellos—son mi hijo y mi amigo—
ascienden la colina
como en busca del trueno y el relámpago.
Yo descanso a la orilla del abismo,
al pie de un mar de vértigos, ahogado
en un inmenso río de helechos doloridos.
Puedo cortar el pensamiento con una espiga,
la voz con un sollozo, o una lágrima,
dormir un infinito dolor, pensar
un amor infinito, una tristeza divina;
mientras ellos, en la suave colina,
sólo encuentran
la dormida raíz de una columna rota
y el eco de un relámpago.

Oh Tajín, oh naufragio,
tormenta demolida,
piedra bajo la piedra;
cuando nadie sea nada y todo quede
mutilado, cuando ya nada sea
y sólo quedes tú, impuro templo desolado,
cuando el país-serpiente sea la ruina y el polvo,
la pequeña pirámide podrá cerrar los ojos
para siempre, asfixiada,
muerta en todas las muertes,
ciega en todas las vidas,
bajo todo el silencio universal
y en todos los abismos.

Tajin, el trueno, el mito, el sacrificio.
Y después, nada.

3

Then the others, my son and my friend,
climb up the hill as if in search
of thunder and lightning.
I rest at the edge of the abyss,
at the foot of the whirling sea,
choked by a huge river of ferns in pain.
I can cut off thought with a knifeblade,
my voice with sobbing or a tear,
I can sleep in endless sorrow,
invent an endless love, a divine sadness;
meanwhile they, on the smooth hillside,
they alone will find
the sleeping root of a broken column
and the echo of a lightning flash.

O Tajín, o tempest,
demolished shipwreck,
stone upon stone;
when nobody is anything and everything
remains dismembered, when nothing really is now
and only you remain, impure desolate temple,
when the serpent-country is all ruins and dust,
the little pyramid will be able to close its eyes
forever, suffocated,
dead among all the dead,
blind among all the living,
under the universal silence
and all abysms.

Tajín: thunder, myth, and sacrifice.
And afterwards, nothing.

DECLARACIÓN DE ODIO

Estar simplemente como delgada carne ya sin piel,
como huesos y aire cabalgando en el alba,
como un pequeño y mustio tiempo
duradero entre penas y esperanzas perfectas.
Estar vilmente atado por absurdas cadenas
y escuchar con el viento los penetrantes gritos
que brotan del océano:
agonizantes pájaros cayendo en la cubierta
de los barcos oscuros y eternamente bellos,
o sobre largas playas ensordecidas, ciegas
de tanta fina espuma como miles de orquídeas.
Porque, ¡qué alto mar, sucio y maravilloso!
Hay olas como árboles difuntos,
hay una rara calma y una fresca dulzura,
hay horas grises, blancas y amarillas.
Y es el cielo del mar, alto cielo con vida
que nos entra en la sangre, dando luz y sustento
a lo que hubiera muerto en las traidoras calles,
en las habitaciones turbias de esta negra ciudad.
Esta ciudad de ceniza y tezontle cada día menos puro,
ciudad de acero, sangre y apagado sudor.

Amplia y dolorosa ciudad donde caben los perros,
la miseria y los homosexuales,
las prostitutas y la famosa melancolía de los poetas,
los rezos y las oraciones de los cristianos.
Sarcástica ciudad donde la cobardía y el cinismo son
        alimento diario
de los jovencitos alcahuetes de talles ondulantes,
de las mujeres asnas, de los hombres vacíos.

Ciudad negra o colérica o mansa o cruel,
o fastidiosa nada más: sencillamente tibia.

DECLARATION OF HATRED

To exist simply like delicate meat without a hide,
like bones and air riding on the dawn,
like a petty and wilted time
endured among sorrows and perfect expectations.
To exist shabbily inhibited by absurd bonds
and to listen with the wind to the piercing screams
that spring up from the ocean:
dying birds falling onto the decks
of dark eternally beautiful ships
or upon long deaf beaches,
blind from so much pure foam like thousands of orchids.
Because the sea is so high, dirty and wonderful!
There are waves like dead trees,
there is a rare calm and a fresh sweetness,
there are grey, white and yellow hours.
And it's the sky above the dead, the tall vivid sky
that enters into our blood, giving light and sustenance
to what had died in the treacherous streets,
and in the confused hotel rooms of this dark city.
This city of ash and volcanic stone less pure every day,
city of pavement, blood and lifeless sweat.

Spacious and sorrowful city where dogs,
misery, homosexuals, prostitutes,
the famous sadness of poets,
prayers and speeches of the Christians fit right in.
Sarcastic city where cowardliness and cynicism
        are daily nourishment
for young gossipers over women's undulating figures,
for silly women and vain men.

Black city or angry city or gentle city or cruel
or boring city; nothing more: simply tepid.

Pero valiente y vigorosa porque en sus calles viven los
días rojos y azules
de cuando el pueblo se organiza en columnas,
los días y las noches de los militantes comunistas,
los días y las noches de las huelgas victoriosas,
los crudos días en que los desocupados adiestran su rencor
agazapados en los jardines o en los quicios dolientes.

¡Los días en la ciudad! Los días pesadísimos
como una cabeza cercenada con los ojos abiertos.
Estos días como frutas podridas.
Días enturbiados por salvajes mentiras.
Días incendiarios en que padecen las curiosas estatuas
y los monumentos son más estériles que nunca.
Larga, larga ciudad con sus albas como vírgenes hipócritas,
con sus minutos como niños desnudos,
con sus bochornosos actos de vieja díscola y aparatosa,
con sus callejuelas donde mueren extenuados, al fin,
los roncos emboscados y los asesinos de la alegría.

Ciudad tan complicada, hervidero de envidias,
criadero de virtudes deshechas al cabo de una hora,
páramo sofocante, nido blando en que somos
como palabra ardiente desoída,
superficie en que vamos como un tránsito oscuro,
desierto en que latimos y respiramos vicios,
ancho bosque regado por dolorosas y punzantes lágrimas,
lágrimas de desprecio, lágrimas insultantes.

Te declaramos nuestro odio, magnífica ciudad.
A ti, a tus tristes y vulgarísimos burgueses,
a tus chicas de aire, caramelos y filmas americanos,
a tus juventudes *ice cream* rellenas de basura,
a tus desenfrenados maricones que devastan
las escuelas, la plaza Garibaldi,
la viva y venenosa calle de San Juan de Letrán.

But bold and vigorous, because in its streets live
the red and blue days
for organizing the people into columns,
the days and nights of militant Communists,
the days and nights of victorious labor strikes,
the crude days in which the unemployed teach their bitterness
crouched down in the gardens or beside doorposts, suffering.

Days in the city! Nightmarish days
like a head sliced off with the eyes open.
Those days like rotten fruit.
Days made muddy on account of savage lies.
Inflammatory days in which the curious statues suffer
and the monuments are more sterile than ever.
Big, big city with its dawns like hypocrite virgins,
its minutes like naked children,
with its thunderous acts of a showy disobedient old woman,
with its narrow streets where the weak,
the ambushed raucous, and the assassins of happiness finally die.

Such a complicated city, seething with desires,
breeding ground for virtues undone at last in a single hour,
stifling bleak wasteland, sensual hotbed in which we're
like a burning disregarded word,
surface upon which we walk as if a dark passageway,
desert upon which we throb and breathe vices,
wide forest watered by sorrows and caustic tears,
scornful tears, insulting tears.

We declare our hatred for you, splendid city.
For you, for your sad and vulgar bourgeoisie,
for your girls made of air, caramels and American films,
for your young ones of ice cream stuffed full of garbage,
for your uncontrolled queers who devastate the schools
and Garibaldi Plaza and the lively poisonous street
        called San Juan Letrán.

Te declaramos nuestro odio perfeccionado a fuerza
de sentirte cada día más inmensa,
cada hora más blanda, cada línea más brusca.
Y si te odiamos, linda, primorosa ciudad sin esqueleto,
no lo hacemos por chiste refinado, nunca por neurastenia,
sino por tu candor de virgen desvestida,
por tu mes de diciembre y tus pupilas secas,
por tu pequeña burguesía, por tus poetas publicistas,
¡por tus poetas, grandísima ciudad!, por ellos y su
        enfadosa categoría de descastados,
por sus flojas virtudes de ocho sonetos diarios,
por sus lamentos al crepúsculo y a la soledad interminable,
por sus retorcimientos histéricos de prometeos sin sexo
o estatuas del sollozo, por su ritmo de asnos en busca
        de una flauta.

Pero no es todo, ciudad de lenta vida.
Hay por ahí escondidos, asustados, acaso masturbándose,
varias docenas de cobardes, niños de la teoría,
de la envidia y el caos, jóvenes del "sentido práctico
        de la vida",
ruines abandonados a sus propios orgasmos,
viles niños sin forma mascullando su tedio,
especulando en libros ajenos a lo nuestro.
¡A lo nuestro, ciudad!, lo que nos pertenece,
lo que vierte alegría y hace florecer júbilos,
risas, risas de gozo de unas bocas hambrientas,
hambrientas de trabajo,
de trabajo y orgullo de ser al fin varones
en un mundo distinto.
Así hemos visto limpias decisiones que saltan
paralizando el ruido mediocre de las calles,
puliendo caracteres, dando voces de alerta,
de esperanza y progreso.

We declare our hatred for you perfected by the force
of feeling you more immense each day,
more bland every hour, more violent every line.
And if we hate you, fine artistic city without skeleton,
we don't do it through a refined joke, never because of
nervous exhaustion, but because of your innocence
       of a naked virgin,
because of your month of December and your dry eyes,
because of your petty bourgeoisie, because of
       your publicist poets,
because of your poets, enormous city! Because of them
and their annoying category as alienated ones,
because of their feeble virtues in eight sonnets daily,
because of their laments in the twilight
and their interminable solitude,
because of their hysterical twistings of sexless promises
or tearful statues, because of their asinine rhythms
       in search of a flute.

But that isn't all, city of slow lifestyles.
There're hidden ones around here, frightened, perhaps
       masturbating,
diverse dozens of cowards, children of theory,
envy and chaos, young ones with a "practical sense of life,"
runts left to their own orgasms,
rotten children without means mumbling about their boredom,
speculating about books alien to what is ours.
To what is ours, city! That which belongs to us,
that which pours forth joy and makes joys flourish:
laughter, joyful laughter from mouths that are hungry,
hungry from work,
from work, and with the pride of finally being worthy men
in a well-defined world.
So we've seen clear judgments leap up
paralyzing the mediocre noise in the streets,
polishing the letters, giving voice to alarm and hope and progress.

Son rosas o geranios, claveles o palomas,
saludos de victoria y puños retadores.
Son las voces, los brazos y los pies decisivos,
y los rostros perfectos, y los ojos de fuego,
y la táctica en vilo de quienes hoy te odian
para amarte mañana cuando el alba sea alba
y no chorro de insultos, y no río de fatigas,
y no una puerta falsa para huir de rodillas.

There are roses or geraniums, carnations or doves,
victory salutes and defiant fists.
There are voices and arms and decisive feet,
and perfect faces, and eyes of fire,
and the tentative tactics of those who hate you now
in order to love you tomorrow when the dawn is the dawn
and not a torrent of insults, and not a river of troubles,
and not a false door for fleeing on one's knees.

AVENIDA JUAREZ

Uno pierde los días, la fuerza y el amor a la patria,
el cálido amor a la mujer cálidamente amada,
la voluntad de vivir, el sueño y el derecho a la ternura;
uno va por ahí, antorcha, paz, luminoso deseo,
deseos ocultos, lleno de locura y descubrimientos,
y uno no sabe nada, porque está dicho que uno no
    debe saber nada,
como si las palabras fuesen los pasos muertos del hambre
o el golpear en el oído de la espesa ola del vicio
o el brillo funeral de los fríos mármoles
o la desnudez angustiosa del árbol
o la inquietud sedosa del agua...

Hay en el aire un río de cristales y llamas,
un mar de voces huecas, un gemir de barbarie,
cosas y pensamientos que hieren;
hay el breve rumor del alba
y el grito de agonía de una noche, otra noche,
todas las noches del mundo
en el crispante vaho de las bocas amargas.

Se camina como entre cipreses,
bajo la larga sombra del miedo,
siempre al pie de la muerte.
Y uno no sabe nada,
porque está dicho que uno debe callar y no saber nada,
porque todo lo que se dice parecen órdenes,
ruegos, perdones, súplicas, consignas.
Uno debe ignorar la mirada de compasión,
caminar por esa selva con el paso del hombre
dueño apenas del cielo que lo ampara,
hablando el español con un temor de siglos,
triste bajo la ráfaga azul de los ojos ajenos,

JUAREZ AVENUE

One wastes away the days, the strength and the love of country,
the warm love of a warmly loving woman,
the will to live, the dream and the right to tenderness;
one goes around there—a torch, peace, brilliant desire,
secret desires filled with madness and revelations,
and one doesn't know anything, because it's said
one doesn't have to know anything,
as if words were the dead footsteps of hunger
or the pounding in the ear of the slovenly wave of vice
or the glittering funeral of the cold marble
or the naked anguish of the tree
or the uneasy silkiness of the water...

There's a river of crystals and flames in the air,
a sea of booming voices, a moan of savagery,
things and thoughts that wound;
there's the brief murmur of the dawn
and the scream of agony of one night, then another night,
all the nights of the world
in the twitching smell of the bitter mouths.

One walks as if among cypress trees,
below a long shadow of fear,
always at the foot of death.
And one doesn't know anything
because it's said one has to keep quiet and not know anything,
because everything that's talked about appears to be orders,
requests, pardons, petitions, instructions.
One has to ignore the compassionate glance,
walk through that jungle with the pace of a man
master of the sky which protects him,
speaking Spanish with a fear of the centuries,
sad under the blue flashes of alien eyes,

enano ante las tribus espigadas,
vencido por el pavor del día y la miseria de la noche,
la hipocresía de todas las almas y, si acaso,
salvado por el ángel perverso del poema y sus alas.

Marchar hacia la condenación y el martirio,
atravesado por las espinas de la patria perdida,
ahogado por el sordo rumor de los hoteles
donde todo se pudre entre mares de whisky y de ginebra.

Marchar hacia ninguna parte, olvidado del mundo,
ciego al mármol de Juárez y su laurel escarnecido
por los pequeños y los grandes canallas;
perseguido por las tibias azaleas de Alabama,
las calientes magnolias de Mississippi,
las rosas salvajes de las praderas
y los políticos pelícanos de Louisiana,
las castas violetas de Illinois,
las *bluebonnets* de Texas...
y los millones de Biblias
como millones de palomas muertas.

Uno mira los árboles y la luz, y sueña
con la pureza de las cosas amadas
y la intocable bondad de las calles antiguas,
con las risas antiguas y el relámpago dorado
de la piel amorosamente dorada por un sol amoroso.
Saluda a los amigos, y los amigos
parecen la sombra de los amigos,
la sombra de la rosa y el geranio,
la desangrada sombra del laurel enlutado.

¿Qué país, que territorio vive uno?
¿Dónde la magia del silencio, el llanto
del silencio en que todo se ama?
(*¿Tantos millones de hombres hablaremos inglés?*)

80

a midget in front of the lanky tribes,
defeated by dread of day and the misery of night,
the hypocrisy of all souls
saved perhaps by the perverse angel of the poem and its wings.

To march toward condemnation and martyrdom,
pierced by the thorns of the lost native land,
choked by the muffled noise in the hotels
where everything rots among seas of gin and whiskey.

To go into any area, forgotten by the world,
blind to the marble on Juarez Avenue and its laurel ridiculed
by tiny and teeming mobs both;
persecuted by the tepid azaleas of Alabama,
the warm magnolias of Mississippi,
the wild roses of the prairies
and the political pelicans of Louisiana,
the incredible violets of Illinois,
the bluebonnets of Texas...
and the millions of Bibles
like millions of dead doves.

One looks at the trees and the light, and dreams
with the purity of cherished things
and the untouchable kindness of the ancient streets,
with the ancient laughter and the golden flash
of the lovingly golden skin because of a loving sun.
One salutes his friends, and friends
appear to be the shadow of friends,
the shadow of the rose and the geranium,
the blood-drowned shadow of the mourned laurel.

What country, what territory does one live in?
Where's the magic in the silence, the weeping
of the silence in which everything loves?
(*How many millions of men will speak English?*)

Uno se lo pregunta
y uno mismo se aleja de la misma pregunta
como de un clavo ardiendo.
Porque todo parece que arde
y todo es un montón de frías cenizas,
un hervidero de perfumados gusanos
en el andar sin danza de las jóvenes,
un sollozar por su destino
en el rostro apagado de los jóvenes,
y un juego con la tumba
en los ojos manchados del anciano.

Todo parece arder, como
una fortaleza tomada a sangre y fuego.
Huele el corazón del paisaje,
el aire huele a pensamientos muertos,
los poetas tienen el seco olor de las estatuas
—y todo arde lentamente
como en un ancho cementerio.

Todo parece morir, agonizar,
todo parece polvo mil veces pisado.
La patria es polvo y carne viva, la patria
debe ser, y no es, la patria
se la arrancan a uno del corazón
y el corazón se lo pisan sin ninguna piedad.

Entonces uno tiene que huir ante el acoso de los búfalos
que todo lo derrumban, ante la furia imperial
del becerro de oro que todo lo ha comprado
—la pequeña república, el pequeño tirano,
los ríos, la energía eléctrica y los bancos—,
y es inútil invocar el nombre de Lincoln
y es por demás volver los ojos a Juárez,
porque a los dos los ha decapitado el hacha

One asks the question
and one moves away from the same question
as if from a burning nail.
Because everything appears to be burning
and everything is a pile of cold ashes,
a seething of sweet-smelling worms
in the danceless walk of young women,
a sob about fate
in the lifeless faces of young men,
and a game with the grave
in the spotted eyes of the old.

Everything appears to burn,
like a fortress overtaken by blood and fire.
The heart smells of the country,
the air smells of dead ideas,
poets possess the dry smell of the statues
and everything burns slowly
as if inside a wide graveyard.

Everything appears to die, agonized;
everything appears to be dust trampled on a thousand times.
The native land is dust and living flesh,
the native land ought to be and isn't, the land—
they started it as one of heart
and trample on the heart without any mercy.

And so one must flee before the relentless pursuit of the
buffaloes who knock over everything, before the imperial rage
of the golden calf which has won over everything
—the little republic, the small-time tyrant,
the rivers, electrical energy and the banks—,
and it's useless to invoke the name of Lincoln
and it's useless to turn one's eyes on Juarez Avenue
because the hatchet has split them in two

y no hay respeto para ninguna paz,
para ningún amor.

No se tiene respeto ni para el aire que se respira
ni para la mujer que se ama tan dulcemente,
ni siquiera para el poema que se escribe.
Pues no hay piedad para la patria,
que es polvo de oro y carne enriquecida
por la sangre sagrada del martirio.

Pues todo parece perdido, hermanos,
mientras amargamente, triunfalmente,
por la Avenida Juárez de la ciudad de México
—perdón, *México City*—
las tribus espigadas, la barbarie en persona,
los turistas adoradores de "Lo que el viento se llevó"
las millonarias neuróticas cien veces divorciadas,
los gángsters y Miss Texas,
pisotean la belleza, envilecen el arte,
se tragan la Oración de Gettysburg y los poemas de
      Walt Whitman,
el pasaporte de Paul Robeson y las películas de
      Charles Chaplin,
y lo dejan a uno tirado a media calle
con los oídos despedazados
y una arrugada postal de Chapultepec
entre los dedos.

and there's no respect for any peace,
for any love.

One doesn't have respect even for the air one breathes;
or for the woman one loves so sweetly,
or for the poem one writes.
Because there's no pity for the native land,
which is gold dust and mineral-rich flesh
because of the sacred blood of martyrdom.

Because everything appears lost, brothers,
while bitterly, triumphantly,
on Juarez Avenue in the city of Mexico
—pardon me, *Mexico City*—
the lanky tribes, the barbarism in person,
the adoring tourists of "what's in the wind today?"
the neurotic millionaires divorced a hundred times,
the gangsters and Miss Texas;
they trample beauty, belittle art,
swallow the Gettysburg Address and the poems of
    Walt Whitman,
the passport of Paul Robeson and the movies of
    Charlie Chaplin,
and they abandon you all at once in the middle of the street
with your ears torn to pieces
and a crumpled postcard from Chapultepec
between your fingers.

DOLORIDO CANTO A LA IGLESIA CATÓLICA Y A QUIENES EN ELLA SUELEN CONFIAR

I

Hermanos míos de raza y sangre, hombres de toda edad,
mujeres de toda belleza y niños de hermoso porvenir,
oídme en esta noche de los diablos,
en esta hora de palomas decapitadas:
La luz es patrimonio del hombre,
del hombre en general y de nuestros hijos
en forma más precisa;
la sabiduría es terreno propicio a la bondad,
y los golpes de pecho son las campanadas del pavor,
los enemigos de la danza y de la primavera.
El cielo y la tierra son propiedad del hombre:
la nube femenina y el masculino surco.
La tierra es ideal para la grata curva de la espiga
y la nube es el sueño de la mujer amada.
La lluvia es nuestra madre tierna y musical.
Música entrecortada de la rosa,
contrapunto maduro del clavel y el geranio,
gentil ballet del nardo y la gladiola.
Todo es bello y perfecto, delicado, purísimo.
Es puro el buen deseo, delicado el amor,
perfecta la mañana, bello el atardecer.
Pero, hermanos, hermanos, oh hermanos
de toda raza y sangre,
oíd cómo de noche, en esta noche de penumbras secas,
murciélagos y tordos desgarran el silencio.
Y la rosa se hiela y el clavel se estremece.
Y todo es como huellas de alba petrificada.

GRIEVING SONG TO THE CATHOLIC CHURCH AND TO THOSE ACCUSTOMED TO TRUSTING HER

I

My brothers of race and blood, men of every age,
women of every beauty and children of a beautiful future,
hear me on this devilish night,
in this hour of beheaded doves:
Light is the birthright of man,
of mankind in general
and of our sons precisely;
wisdom is earthly success with kindness,
and blows to the chest are the ringing out of dread,
the enemies of dance and of spring.
The sky and the earth are the property of man:
the womanly cloud and the manly furrow.
The earth is perfect for the pleasing curve of an ear of wheat
and a cloud is the dream of a loving woman.
The earth is our mother, tender and musical.
Intermittent music from the rose,
ripe counterpoint of the carnation and the geranium,
graceful ballet of the spikenard and the gladiola.
All is beautiful and perfect, delicate, most pure.
The good intention is pure; delicate love,
a perfect tomorrow, a beautiful nightfall.
But brothers, brothers, oh brothers
of every race and blood,
listen how in the night, in this night of dry shadows,
bats and thrushes shatter the silence.
And the rose freezes and the carnation shakes.
And everything is like footprints of a petrified dawn.

II

Bendito sea el temor escalofriante.
Y bendito tu nombre, Jesucristo, varón a sangre y fuego,
látigo y maldición. Bendito sea tu nombre, como maldito es,
bajo el polvo de siglos, el crujir de sotanas
(águilas de rencor y de lascivia);
como maldito es
el amargo murmullo de los rezos;
como maldito es el vaho tremendamente sepulcral del incensario;
como maldito es en esta tierra el horrendo lebrel
que a dinamita pura vuela el templo evangélico.
Bendito seas, hermoso Jesucristo a la orilla del lago,
y santa tu palabra de bondad y miseria.
Pero maldito sea quien en tu nombre alzó
la cruz del latrocinio, y tus bellas espinas subastó en el mercado.

Un Jehová melancólico contempla la tragedia,
vuestra estéril tragedia, sacerdotes del miedo
que pisáis la engañosa ceniza bajo la cual el fuego
va señalando rutas y destinos torcidos;
vuestra fría tragedia donde el Bautista se ahoga
y el joven Sebastián multiplica sus flechas;
vuestra frenética tragedia de cirios verdes y crespones negros
roídos por la anciana del atrio y los intelectuales tragahostias.
Pero un momento, hermanos, un momento tan sólo,
para escuchar la voz, la plegaria monjil,
la cuchillada mortal a los espíritus:
"Vivan tus ángeles aquí para conservarnos en paz,
y sea tu bendición siempre sobre nosotros
por Cristo Nuestro Señor. Amén".
Y es entonces, hermanos, cuando las catedrales tiemblan,
y sobre la iglesuca y en torno a la Basílica de la Señora que sabéis,
alienta brutalmente el amarillo de niebla de las hipocresías,

II

Blessed be the chilling fear.
And blessed your name, Jesus Christ, great one of blood and fire,
whips and curses. Blessed be your name,
as beneath the dust of centuries, the creak of cassocks
(eagles of ill will and lewdness)
is damned;
as the bitter whispering of the prayers is damned;
as the gloomy smell of the incense ritual is damned;
as damned as on earth the frightful greyhound is
who with pure dynamite demolishes the evangelical temple.
Blessed be you, handsome Jesus Christ by the side of the lake,
and holy be your word of kindness and misery.
But damned be the ones who in your name
raised the cross of robbery, and auctioned off
your beautiful thorns in the marketplace.

A sad Jehovah contemplates the tragedy,
your sterile tragedy, priests full of fear
who scatter false ash under which the fire
goes on pointing out twisted roads and fates;
your cold tragedy where Baptist is drowned
and young Sebastian multiplies his arrows;
your frantic tragedy of green candles and black crepe
gnawed upon by the old woman in the inner courtyard
and by the intellectual gluttons.
Yet one time, brothers, one time only,
heed the voice, the nun's supplication,
the mortal slash to the spirits:
"Your angels live here to preserve us in peace,
and may your blessing forever be upon us
through our Lord Christ, Amen."
And it's then, brothers, that the cathedrals tremble,
and above the church and around the Basilica of the Lady
the yellow mist of hypocrisies brutally breathes, you know,

y el temor al Infierno desgrana los serviles rosarios,
y el sudor fraterniza con el agua bendita,
y los sucios mercaderes de la fe se refugian
en el rincón más sórdido de su conciencia.
Y mientras, por las calles, un automóvil cruza
        cual espectro del vicio,
y en él, el Arzobispo, sonrientemente feo y satisfecho.

                    III

Llevamos 6000 años de creer en el destino de las estrellas.
Lo sabe el Santo Padre, lo sabe Merle Oberon,
lo sienten en carne viva los viejos judíos que
        agonizan al pie del muro.
Y sin embargo, oh hermanos, "la espada del
        Señor está llena de sangre.
Se ha hartado de las grasas de los riñones de los carneros".
Y vosotros, sacerdotes, arzobispos, criminales curas de pueblo,
histéricos cuervos de la colonia San Rafael,
envenenados habitantes del mal,
os bebéis las lágrimas congeladas de un Cristo mutilado,
seguís distrayendo la moneda del artesano,
tomáis al hombre, ensombreciéndolo,
        entristeciéndolo para siempre,
y lo dejáis a media calle, deshecho, con una
piedra de terror hundida en el alma.
El Día de la Ira rendiréis cuentas claras...
Y ese Día es, felizmente, todos los días, todas las horas
de este país nuestro que vosotros martirizáis sin descanso,
expoliándolo, carcomiéndolo lentamente hasta las llagas.
Sois malditos por naturaleza. Pequeños y
grandes malditos de corazón,
habéis traicionado a la Patria un millón de veces
y todavía sonreís y clamáis al cielo y a los banqueros.
Pero no habrá perdón para vosotros, jamás

and the fear of Hell removes the grains
    from the servile rosary beads
and sweat fraternizes with the holy water,
and the dirty merchants of the faith take refuge
in the most sordid corner of your conscience.
Meanwhile an automobile crosses through the streets
    like a specter of vice
and in it is the Archbishop grinningly hideous and satisfied.

III

We bear 6,000 years of belief in the destiny of the stars.
The Holy Father knows it, Merle Oberon knows it,
the old Jews dying at the foot of the wall
sense it in the living flesh.
And still, oh brothers, "the Lord's sword
is full of blood. It's been sated
on the fat of the kidneys of sheep."
And you! Priests, archbishops, criminal curates of the people,
hysterical crows of the San Rafael colony,
poisoned residents of evil,
you yourselves drink the frozen tears of a mutilated Christ,
you go on diverting the coins of the craftsman,
you drink to man overshadowing him, saddening him forever,
and you abandon him in the middle of the street,
shattered, with a stone of terror sunken in his soul.
On the Day of Judgment you'll be called to account...
And that Day is, fortunately, every day,
every hour in this country of ours
which you'd martyrize relentlessly,
exploiting it, wasting it slowly until it ulcerates.
May you be damned by nature. You big
and little perverters of heart
have betrayed your native land a million times
and still you smile and cry out to the sky and to the bankers.
But there won't be any mercy for you, never

    habrá perdón para vosotros,
asesinos de la luz, cercenadores de la piedad,
máscaras del embuste, fabricantes de lascivia.
No habrá perdón para vosotros,
no habrá perdón para vosotros,
no habrá perdón para vosotros.

any mercy for you,
assassins of the light, amputators of pity,
masqueradors of fraud, manufacturers of lust.
There won't be any mercy for you,
there won't be any mercy for you,
there won't be any mercy for you.

DESPLIEGUE DE ASOMBROS
ANTE UN DIOS

Lo primero es el cielo. Después viene
el espléndido dios que todo lo atruena
con su nariz agujereada y sus miembros
comidos por el hambre de siglos.

El dios vivo y marcado, ungido
con cenizas y lágrimas en cada poro.
El dios traído a un templo a través de otros
templos y otras catedrales y otros misterios.

El dios puesto de pie, venerado,
herido de dolor y de miseria.

Oh dios de cielos y caminos, dios
de agua y furor, dios maldito de misericordia,
devóranos con tu boca sin labios
y tu dura palabra de serpientes heladas.

Oh sordo, ciego y luminoso dios,
enciende alguna vez el rostro del pueblo,
de este bosque sin dueño, propiedad
de todos y de nadie. Patria de espejos
y mediodías, patria embriagada de muerte.

Húndela, inúndela, oh dios sacado
del secreto, dios que miró abrirse
vientres mestizos y padeció la primera herradura.

UNFURLING OF AMAZEMENTS
BEFORE GOD

The first thing is the sky. After that comes
the magnificent god who stuns everybody
with his perforated nose and his limbs
eaten by the hunger of centuries.

The living and marked god,
anointed with ashes and tears in every pore.
The ragged god in a temple across from other temples
and other cathedrals and other mysteries.

The god standing upright, venerated,
wounded by pain and poverty.

Oh god of skies and roads, god
of water and passion, god cursed by forgiveness,
devour us with your lipless mouth
and your harsh words made of frozen snakes.

Oh deaf, blind, luminous god,
light up the face of the nation
in this forest without a landlord,
the property of everybody and nobody. Country of mirrors
and 12 o'clock noons, country drunk on death.

Destroy it, flood it out, oh god pulled loose
from the secret, god who watched mestizo guts open
and who suffered the first horseshoe.

RÍO SAN LORENZO

Un río lleno de cielos,
un río lleno de nubes,
un río lleno de estelas,
un río lleno de verdes,
lleno de alas, lleno de ángeles;
un río anchamente dulce,
un río lleno de adioses,
un río para mirarse,
un río para morirse,
un río para vivir,
lleno de ansias, lleno de sueños,
lleno de arboles, lleno de junio,
lleno de sol, lleno de alba,
lleno de rosas y palomas.

THE SAN LORENZO RIVER

A river full of skies,
a river full of clouds,
a river full of trails,
a river full of greens,
full of wings, full of angels;
a wide gentle river,
a river full of good-byes,
a river to contemplate deeply,
a river for dying in,
and a river for living in,
full of anguish, full of dreams,
full of trees, full of June,
full of sunlight, full of daylight,
full of roses and doves.

LOS HOMBRES DEL ALBA

Y después, aquí, en el oscuro seno del río más oscuro,
en lo más hondo y verde de la vieja ciudad,
estos hombres tatuados: ojos como diamantes,
bruscas bocas de odio más insomnio,
algunas rosas o azucenas en las manos
y una desesperante ráfaga de sudor.

Son los que tienen en vez de corazón
un perro enloquecido
o una simple manzana luminosa
o un frasco con saliva y alcohol
o el murmullo de la una de la mañana
o un corazón como cualquiera otro.

Son los hombres del alba.
Los bandidos con la barba crecida
y el bendito cinismo endurecido,
los asesinos cautelosos
con la ferocidad sobre los hombros,
los maricas con fiebre en las orejas
y en los blandos riñones,
los violadores,
los profesionales del desprecio,
los del aguardiente en las arterias,
los que gritan, aúllan como lobos
con las patas heladas.
Los hombres más abandonados,
más locos, más valientes:
los más puros.

Ellos están caídos de sueño y esperanzas,
con los ojos en alto, la piel gris
y un eterno sollozo en la garganta.

THE MEN OF DAWN

And later, here, in the dark heart of the darkest river,
in the old city's greenest depth,
these tattooed men: eyes like diamonds,
foul mouths of hatred plus insomnia,
some roses or lilies in their hands
and a desperate blast of sweat.

Those who have a mad dog
in place of a heart
or a simple polished apple
or a flask of alcohol and spit
or a moan at one in the morning
or a heart like anyone else.

They are the men of dawn.
Bandits with their heavy beards
and simple hard-core cynicism,
the careful assassins
with ferocity atop their shoulders,
queers with fever in their ears
and in their delicate guts,
the violators,
the professional scorners,
with raw brandy in their veins,
those who howl and shout like wolves
with frozen paws.
The most abandoned,
crazy brave
and pure ones.

They've fallen from dreams and hopes,
with their eyes open, with cloudy skin
and an endless sob in their throat.

Pero hablan. Al fin la noche es una misma
siempre, y siempre fugitiva:
es un dulce tormento, un consuelo sencillo,
una negra sonrisa de alegría,
un modo diferente de conspirar,
una corriente tibia temerosa
de conocer la vida un poco envenenada.
Ellos hablan del día. Del día,
que no les pertenece, en que no se pertenecen,
en que son más esclavos; del día,
en que no hay más camino
que un prolongado silencio
o una definitiva rebelión.

Pero yo sé que tienen miedo del alba.
Sé que aman la noche y sus lecciones escalofriantes.
Sé de la lluvia nocturna cayendo
como sobre cadáveres.
Sé que ellos construyen con sus huesos
un sereno monumento a la angustia.
Ellos y yo sabemos estas cosas:
que la gemidora metralla nocturna,
después de alborotar brazos y muertes,
después de oficiar apasionadamente
como madre del miedo,
se resuelve en rumor,
en penetrante ruido,
en cosa helada y acariciante,
en poderoso árbol con espinas plateadas,
en reseca alambrada:
en alba. En alba
con eficacia de pecho desafiante.

Entonces un dolor desnudo y terso
aparece en el mundo.
Y los hombres son pedazos de alba,

But they speak... In the end, the night is
always the same transitory miasma,
it's a sweet torment, a simple consolation,
a black smile of joy,
another way of conspiring,
a lukewarm, timid way
of finding life slightly poisoned.
They speak of the day... The day,
which isn't theirs, and where they don't belong,
in which they're slaves, the day
which has no path
except a long silence
or a final rebellion.

But I know they're afraid of the dawn.
I know they love the night and its chilling lessons.
I know the rain falling at night
as if falling on corpses.
I know with their bones they make
a serene monument to anguish.
Together we know this:
that the wailing bullets of the night,
after inciting the riot of arms and death,
after passionately officiating
as a mother of fear,
settle into murmurs
and piercing noise,
into something frozen and caressing,
into a powerful tree with silver thorns,
into tangled barbed wire,
into dawn. Into a dawn
which affects us like a rebellious heart.

Then a clear and naked sorrow
appears in the world.
And men are pieces of dawn,

son tigres en guardia,
son pájaros entre hebras de plata,
son escombros de voces.
Y el alba negrera se mete en todas partes:
en las raíces torturadas,
en las botellas estallantes de rabia,
en las orejas amoratadas,
en el húmedo desconsuelo de los asesinos,
en la boca de los niños dormidos.

Pero los hombres del alba se repiten
en forma clamorosa,
y ríen y mueren como guitarras pisoteadas,
con la cabeza limpia
y el corazón blindado.

tigers on guard,
birds upon silver strings,
the remainders of voices.
And the blackened dawn plunges down everywhere:
into the tortured roots,
into bottles bursting with rage,
into bruised and beaten ears,
into the damp sorrow of assassins,
into the mouths of sleeping children.

But the men of dawn shout
the same way as always,
and they laugh and die like trampled guitars,
with their helmetless skulls
and armor-plated hearts.

LA DONCELLA

Verde
Que te
Quiero
Verde
Verde
Viejo
Viejo
Verde
    A qué
    Horas
    Vas
    A
    Llegar?

THE VIRGIN

Green
That's what
I want
Green
Green
Ancient
Ancient
Green
    What time
    are you going
    to arrive?

DESCONCIERTO

A mis
Viejos
Maestros
De marxismo
No los puedo
Entender:
Unos están
En la cárcel
Otros están
En el
Poder

CONFUSION

As for
my old
teachers
of Marxism
I don't
understand them:
Some are
in prison
others are
in power.

OMINOSA

Lo satánico
Y antidialéctico
Es que
En la lucha
Armada
Son *ellos*
Los que
Tienen
Las armas

OMINOUS THOUGHT

The satanic
and antidialectical
is that
in the armed
struggle
it's *they*
who have
the arms

MANSA HIPÉRBOLE

Los lunes, miércoles y viernes
Soy un indigente sexual;
Lo mismo que los martes,
Los jueves y los sábados.

Los domingos descanso.

TAME HYPERBOLE

Mondays, Wednesdays, and Fridays
I am a sexual native;
The same is true on Tuesdays,
Thursdays and Saturdays.

On Sundays I rest.

CHE

Para Eugenia Huerta

En
La
Calle
Deben
Pasar
Cosas
Extraordinarias

Por
Ejemplo
La
    REVOLUCIÓN

CHE

for Eugenia Huerta

Extraordinary
Things
Ought to
Come
Down
The
Street

For
Example
The
    REVOLUTION.

PROBLEMA DEL ALMA

I

Alma mía, sin verte,
sin oírte latir sobre la piel
ni en lo profundo de la negra sangre,
esta sangre que no debía ignorarte como yo,
esta sangre tan mía y tan ajena,
como tú, alma gris de pesadumbre,
alma de lejanía, tan blanda.
Y sin verte, alma mía,
mi sueño disecado
es una rosa huérfana,
una brasa cansada, dolorida,
triste músculo frío, lacerado
por crueles, crueles lluvias
y llantos errabundos.

Alma mía, sin verte,
sin oírte latir sobre mi piel
        —!qué conquista tan breve!—,
sin ruidos ni silencios,
sin quebrarme la angustia,
mírame con tus ojos, dolorida,
desgárrame los huesos, gran ausente,
alma gris, verde o clara, mi enemiga,
mi dueña, madre de mi fatiga.

Pero lo sé. Aquí estás,
substancia poderosa,
suave viento de marzo,
en mis manos abiertas,
aquí estás.

PROBLEMS OF THE SOUL

I

Soul of mine, without seeing you,
without hearing you throb against my skin
nor in the depths of my dark blood,
this blood which couldn't ignore you as I did,
this blood so very mine and so very alien,
like you, gray sorrowful soul,
distant soul, so delicate.
And without seeing you, my soul,
my dissected dream
is an orphaned rose,
a burned-out coal tender and sore,
a sad cold muscle sliced up
by cruelties, cruel rains
and errant tears.

Soul of mine, without seeing you,
without hearing you throb against my skin
    —such a very brief conquest—
without sounds nor silence,
without anxiety breaking me,
look at me with your eyes,
painfully,
shatter my bones, great absent one,
gray soul, green or clear, my enemy,
my master, mother of my weariness.

But I know. Here you are,
powerful essence,
gentle March breeze
through my open hands,
here you are.

Me duele tu contacto, triunfadora,
como al viento le duele
la esencia de los pájaros,
bandera, oh invulnerable,
tan fuerte y misteriosa.

Sí, me dueles: en sueños que son ríos,
en pensamientos infecundos,
en el negro sudor de las blasfemias,
en los días minerales, alma mía,
y en el amor que flota en mi memoria
y en mis lágrimas de libertad
como un aceite, o mejor, como un rocío.

Y sin verte, enemiga,
sin saber si eres música
o simplemente niebla.
Dejándome perder forma y sentidos,
dejándome morir entre fauces de lobos,
cruda espuma de canes y duros huesos de alas.

?Qué sueños pueden ser, alma, los míos,
si tú no los alientas con tus ojos?
?Cómo entonces vivir, con qué dedos tocar
el rostro de los niños si en mi piel generosa
no lates, alma mía, con suave desconsuelo
y llanto de bondad?

II

Una noche de lluvia,
entre penumbras,
oí tus grises pasos,
alma mía:
sentí que grandes plumas,

Your touch hurts me, victorious one,
like the wind hurts
the essence of birds,
oh invincible banner,
so strong and mysterious.
Yes, you hurt me: in dreams which are rivers,
in sterile thoughts,
in the dark toil of insults,
 in the mineral days, soul of mine,
and in the love which floats in my memory,
and in my tears of liberty
like an oil, or better, like dew.

And without seeing you, my enemy,
without knowing if you're music
or simply mist.
Letting me lose form and senses,
letting me die in jaws of wolves,
crude spittle of hounds and brittle wing bones.

What can dreams be, my soul
if you don't inspire them with your eyes?
How then to live, with what fingers to touch
the faces of children if within my generous skin
 you don't throb, soul of mine, with a gentle sadness
and a grieving for kindness?

II

A rainy night
among shadows;
I heard your gray footsteps,
soul of mine:
I felt as if large feathers,

que millares de hojas
me rodeaban, atándome,
llagándome tan dulce,
tan dulcísimamente
que aún me miro la piel
como si en ella
se hubiesen dado cita
suaves brisas y agujas,
senos de seda y dedos
como leche caliente.
Quise tocar tu rostro,
y en mis manos quedaron
fragmentos de mi sueño
y un temblor de misterio;
quise coger tus manos
y en las mías, como aliento,
hubo tan sólo un eco
de música divina;
quise llorar, y el llanto
fue apenas la promesa
de unas lágrimas turbias;
quise, entonces, gemir
con angustia de bestia,
o gritar como niño,
pero de mi garganta
sólo brotó una ráfaga
de árbol martirizado.

Pero en mi piel, tu huella
es como el signo mágico
del más alto secreto.

as if thousands of leaves
surrounded me, clinging to me,
wounding me so sweetly,
so very very sweetly,
that I even perceived my skin
as if soft breezes and needles
had passed over it,
breasts of silk and fingers
like warm milk.
I wanted to touch your face,
and in my hands
fragments of my dream
and a rumbling mystery remained;
I wanted to hold your hands
and in mine, like breath,
only an echo of heavenly music
was held.
I wanted to cry, and crying
was hardly a pledge
of cloudy tears;
then I wanted to howl
with the anguish of a wild animal
or scream like a child,
but from my throat
only a burst
of a tortured tree came forth.

But inside my skin, your imprint
is like a magical symbol
of the highest secret.

III

Por la triste hazaña del agua que no corre,
por esta suave astilla que me hiere,
dame, joven virtuosa,
el reposo en la vida
la evidencia del alba,
la línea de la nube;
dame, joven oleaje,
mía, palpable,
el secreto vivaz de la espesura,
del alma vegetal,
y róbame un jazmín,
tan poderoso
como un raudal de llanto.

Pero no me distraigas
ni hables con los espejos,
oh tú, mi esbelto azar,
que soy el alma,
esto es, lo sobrehumano.

Pues más allá del hombre
está el relieve gris:
la fatiga del muro carcomido,
la vida íntima de los herbazales,
la niña brisa y el sudor del césped,
y el misterio que suena,
que refleja la eternidad
y el doloroso enigma
de las lágrimas.

III

Because of the sad fact that water doesn't run,
because of this smooth splinter that wounds me,
give me, young virtuous one,
rest in this life,
proof of the dawn,
the outline of a cloud;
give me, young surging one,
mine, palpable,
the lasting secret of wild thickets,
of the vegetal soul,
and steal me a jasmine
so very powerful
like a flood of tears.

But don't distract me
nor tell me by way of mirrors
oh you, my willowy fate,
that I'm the soul,
this is, superhuman.

So beyond man
there's a gray dimension:
the weariness of a decayed wall,
the intimate life of the grasslands,
the young breeze and the dampness of grass,
the mystery which rings out
and reflects eternity
and the powerful enigma
of tears.

IV

Una pluma de fuego,
eso es el alma;
una distancia, y sed,
eso es el alma;
rayo de sol, y grito,
eso es el alma.

Nadie, seguramente,
lo sabía.
Ni la muchacha que usa
como falda una nube,
ni el jazmín.
Era triste ignorarlo
y vivir,
latir como una orquídea
   —la flor loca—,
sin sentido.

!Ancha herida sin fin,
eso es el alma!
El alma, la insegura,
la absorbente,
la gran pluma de fuego,
el agudo morir,
la vida en bruto.

V

En tu semblante de vegetal en reposo, joven mía,
una breve moneda y sal de miedo gimen
frente a mi blando corazón sin sangre,
!sin la gozosa sangre decisiva!
sin esa sangre, niña de mi sueño.

IV

A plume of fire,
that's the soul;
a distant thing and thirst,
that's the soul;
a ray of sun and a scream,
that's the soul.

Nobody knew it
for sure.
Not the girl who wears
a cloud for a skirt,
nor the jasmine.
It was sad not to know it
and to live,
to pulsate like an orchid
   —that wild flower—
without feeling.

A deep endless wound,
that's the soul!
The soul: uncertain,
all absorbing,
a great plume of fire,
a painful dying,
raw life.

V

In your vegetal countenance in repose, my girl,
a brief sign and recognition of fear are moaning
before my soft bloodless heart
without the joyous blood decisive!
without that blood, child of my dream.

En mis acartonadas manos sin laureles
    —viejas ramas tranquilas,
       herbazales en calma—,
en el resignado surco de mi tacto,
la fiel ternura ciega,
promesa de la muerte,
duerme su poderío,
y en esta ociosa
 tierra gris de mis huesos,
quiero decir, del alma,
no hay sosiego,
sólo esquivas cenizas
o gemidos.
En tu semblante de amor la prodigiosa orilla
del triunfo se palpa, y un ruiseñor de arena
y un peregrino llanto se extravían.
Tu tierna zozobra es una brisa insegura
en doloroso cauce de tinieblas.
Pero el alma, la sobria, la terrenal y lánguida,
?en qué misterio de aire es un secreto
or una ola resuelta en soplo vigilante?
(!Ah los huesos cortantes, los agresivos, fríos!
Cristales sin espíritu, astillas infecundas.)

En mi corazón de madera húmeda
-mi corazón a expensas de la niebla-
una gota de sangre es la ternura
y un latido es oleaje de amarilla,
cálida pesadumbre, o un rumor
de muerte sin relieve ni espesura.

La angustia, la creadroa, no me dice
ni una palabra, o himno. Un vaho
de lejanos perfiles, noche y día
me desvela; no he descubierto aún
por qué la pulsadora

In my shriveled laurel-less hands
    —old motionless branches,
        like quiet grasslands—
in the resigned wrinkle of my touch,
the loyal blind tenderness,
a promise of death,
your power sleeps,
and in this fallow
gray earth of my bones,
I mean, of the soul,
there is no peace,
only elusive ashes
or moans.
On your countenance of love the prodigious shore
of triumph is felt, and a nightingale of sand
and a stray sorrow are missing.
Your tender anxiety is an uncertain breeze
in a painful riverbed of darkness.
But the soul, the sober, earthy and languid one
in what mystery of air is a secret
or a wave, resolved in the twinkling of an eye?
(Oh, the sharp-edged bones, the aggressive ones, so cold!
Crystals without spirit, sterile splinters!)

In my heart of damp wood
-my heart at the expense of the mist-
a drop of blood is the tenderness
and a heartbeat is the surge of yellow,
a warm sorrow, or a murmur
of death without dimension or substance.

My anguish, the creative self, tells me
not a single word, nor a hymn. A mist
of distant silhouettes keeps me awake
night and day; I haven't yet discovered
why the pulsating ashes are fruitless,

ceniza no es un fruto,
un reflejo,
ni cuándo de la dicha necesaria
podrá nacer lo último:
la evidencia del alba.

Decía que en tu semblante de amor...
Pero si ya no oyes: un anillo
de lamentos y lágrimas te cerca.
A la altura del caos
una mano sutil es un presagio.
Parece que morir es encontrarse
desnudo, derramado en un estío
de distancias y gritos y dulzuras.

a reflection,
nor when, from the happiness we need,
can be born the utmost truth:
proof of the dawn.

It's been said that in your countenance of love...
But if you can no longer hear: a ring of sorrows and tears
surrounds you.
At the height of chaos
a gentle hand is an omen.
It seems that to die is to find oneself
naked, squandered in a summer
of distances and screams and sweetness.

LA TRAICÍON GENERAL

No; no era verdad tanta limpia belleza.
No es la primavera un retumbar de vivas al mediodía
o un canto exaltado al mito del paisaje
como dispensador exclusivo de virtudes y glorias;
no son el vellocino de oro los crepúsculos
ni el arcoíris una cesta de manzanas y sonrisas;
tampoco es el amor esa linda promesa
que todavía entre penas y oraciones
ronda por los jardines y muere sollozando;
no son la soledad, la ausencia y el silencio,
las lágrimas y el tedio ciertas flojas nociones
impuestas a millares de alabanzas, sino ruines
y desquiciantes formas de soborno,
vergonzante sistema para frenar impulsos.
Y ahora, cuando nada nos pasa desapercibido,
denunciamos a los traidores, a los huecos poetas
que nos cantaron "nanas" deliberadamente
y nos dieron calmantes y narcóticos
distrayendo atenciones y ennegreciendo vidas.
Ahora vemos todo en recio primer término:
Alberti, Pla y Beltrán, Manuel Altolaguirre,
Gil-Albert, Rosa Chacel, Raúl González Tuñón,
Serrano Plaja y otros notifican al mundo
que la sangre es autora de las albas perfectas,
de nuestra fe social, de los claros crepúsculos,
del coraje vibrante de los "monos" azules,
que la sangre derramada y la robusta tierra
alimentan la furia de un pueblo que combate,
de un pueblo con sus vísceras y nervios como rocas.
Porque no hay más verdad, porque no hay más belleza
que la expuesta y vivida interviniendo

WIDESPREAD BETRAYAL

No; so much pure beauty wasn't truth.
Spring is not resounding cheers at noon
or a passionate song about the myth of the landscape
as the single source of virtues and glories.
Sunsets are not golden fleece
nor is the rainbow a basket of apples and smiles;
nor is love that pretty little promise
which still prowls through the gardens
amid sorrows and political speeches
and then dies weeping;
it's not the solitude, the sense of loss, the silence
the tears or the tedium which certain cowardly ideas
bring out in thousands of eulogies, but the heartless
disgusting forms of bribery
inside a shamefaced system
which rubs out any impulsive actions.
And now, when nothing passes by unnoticed,
we denounce the traitors, the pompous poets
who've deliberately sung us bedtime songs
and given us downers and other dope too
distracting attentions and darkening lives.
Now we suddenly see everything up front:
Alberti, Pla y Beltrán, Manuel Altolaguirre,
Gil-Albert, Rosa Chacel, Raúl González Tuñon,
Serrano Plaja and others send a message to the world
that bloodshed is the creator of perfect dawns,
of our loyalty to society, of crystal clear sunsets,
of the vibrant fighting spirit of the "blue-jeaned" workers;
that bloodshed and the tough old earth
add fuel to the fury of the people who revolt,
people with guts and with nerves of stone.
Because there's no higher truth, no higher beauty
than the lively and dangerous participation

en el fiero conflicto que alborota los climas
quebrando el rostro de los indiferentes,
de los puros, de los que prohijaron fríamente
la traición general, la farsa del silencio.

in the fiery struggle which shakes up the status quo
contorts the faces of the apathetic ones,
of the squeaky clean ones, of those who flat-out adopt
the widespread betrayal, the farce of silence.

CANTATA PARA EL CHE GUEVARA

Andaba suelta la amarilla muerte de ciegos ojos,
de ciegos ojos la amarilla muerte andaba suelta.
Agrios pasos azules en medio del follaje y el fango.
Agria y espesa muerte buscadora, mortalmente buscona.
Gran muerte, grande y maldita muerte, feroz perseguidora.
Andaba suelta aquella muerte tuya, aquella dentellada,
aquellas balas, aquel verde-gusano de las boinas verdes.
Suelta andaba la muerte aquel dia de las balas
y tus pies lastimados y tus cabellos ultrajados
y tu reseca voz de follajes malditamente mutilados.
Si dijiste *Déjenme vivir. Para ustedes*
valgo más vivo que muerto, te respondieron las blasfemias
y las hojas más altas de los pinares volaron al cielo,
porque siempre te cuidaba una parvada de palomas
y tus palabras de amor eran orquídeas y mariposas
para la sintaxis impecable de nuestro claro porvenir.
Andaba suelta como una jauría aquella muerte tuya,
Che Guevara. Suelta andaba con sus pasos de plomo.
Con sus pasos de plomo suelta andaba la muerte, Che Guevara.
Había plomo en la boca del delator y del traidor,
y barranca arriba subía un río de plomo y de miedo.
La boina verde andaba a la caza de la orquídea salvaje
y el helicóptero buscaba con furia a la mariposa.
Aquella muerte verdinegra te asediaba en la escaramuza
y en los hombres tuyos prisioneros y torturados.
Por el hocico del gorila salía la negra muerte
y era tu muerte lo que sudaban los mercenarios.
Los ríos llevaban en su lomo la espuma de tu muerte
y había sangre tuya en las heladas cresterías.
Ya te teníamos muerto en nuestras venas de agonizantes
y una noche la guillotina nos cortó el habla y el sueño.
Te sabíamos rodeado, aislado, enfurecido y triste
como el último capitán de nuestra esperanza,

CANTATA FOR CHE GUEVARA

The yellow death with blind eyes was being released,
with blind eyes the yellow death was being released.
Bitter blue footprints in the jungle and the mud.
And a bitter and dirty, searching and mortally prostitute death.
A huge death, a huge wicked death, a fierce persecutor.
That death of yours was being released, that toothmark,
those bullets, that green worm of the green berets.
Death that day from the bullets was being released
with your wounded feet and your outraged hair
and your hungry voice in the wickedly dismembered jungle brush.
If you said to them "Let me live. I'm worth more to you alive
than dead," blasphemies would have answered you
and the leaves high in the pine groves fly to the sky
because a flock of doves always took care of you
and your words of love were orchids and butterflies
for the impeccable syntax of our bright future.
That death of yours was being released like a pack of hounds,
Che Guevara. Was being released with its steps of lead.
With its steps of lead, death was being released, Che Guevara.
There's lead in the mouth of the accuser and the traitor,
and a steep canyon carries away a river of lead and fear.
The green berets go hunting for the wild orchid
and helicopters search furiously for the butterfly.
That greenish-black death surrounded you
and your imprisoned and tortured men in battle.
From your gorilla mug the black death leaped out
and it was your death which mercenaries sweated for.
Rivers were carrying the froth of your death in their spines
and your blood in the freezing rapids.
Now your death takes hold in our dying veins
and one night guillotines will chop off our speech and our dreams.
We will know you surrounded, isolated, furious and sad
as the peerless commander of our hopes, Che Guevara.

Che Guevara. De aquella esperanza de dulces verdes
bolivarianos, de verdes mexicanos y de verdes hermanos.
Las pequeñas y grandes patrias se estremecieron
con los irremediables disparos que te dieron la muerte,
y luego, dicen, te cercenaron los dedos,
y después, asegura el sanguinario mayor, te llevaron
a lo desconocido para quemar tu cuerpo
y convertirlo en las cenizas infinitas de nuestro amor,
Che Guevara cargado de la muerte de los siglos,
Che Guevara padre e hijo de la independencia,
nieto de todas las libertades de todo el mundo,
forjador de poemas, hacedor de futuros.
Así que aquella muerte te encontró, la encontraste,
y así las balas te lastimaron de muerte
y una selvática oscuridad recorrió cordilleras, colinas,
pampas, llanuras, desiertos, bosques, mares, ríos...
Oh comandante herido y muerto, oh comandante llorado
hasta no sabemos, sí sabemos cuándo y a qué hora.
En la precisa hora de tu muerte sonó la hora
    de nuestra libertad.

18 de noviembre de 1967

134

The hopes of gentle young Bolivians, of young Mexicans
and of all young comrades.
Small and large countries tremble
with uncontrolled gunfire which killed you
and then, they say, they cut off your fingers and toes
and afterward they captured the blood-thirsty mayor,
they took you away to a hidden place to burn your body
and change it into the eternal ashes of our love.
Che Guevara, loaded with the death of centuries,
Che Guevara, father and child of independence,
grandson of all the liberties of the entire world,
creator of poems, maker of futures.
The result is that death met you, and you faced death
and the bullets of death wounded you,
and a wild darkness surged over mountaintops, hillsides,
grasslands, deserts, valleys, forests, oceans, and rivers...
Oh wounded and dead commandante, oh mourned commandante,
we don't even know exactly when and at what hour.
But at the precise moment of your death
    the time of our liberty rang out.

November 18, 1967

ESTO SE LLAMA LOS INCENDIOS

Cuatro jinetes de pólvora derriten los vastos jardines.
Cuatro fantasmas de plomo cavan la tumba del amor.
Uno, dos, tres, innumerables asesinos decapitan
    el ángel de la dicha.
Un jinete de enrojecidos ojos cabalga los incendios.
Algo como una lejana tristeza sucede allá,
en el país de las praderas, del napalm, del oro y
    de los enormes ríos
que de pronto se alzan y se preguntan qué pasa,
aló aló qué ocurre en las ciudades de mármol,
en las ciudades de miasma; ¿qué sucede que se ha roto
el coloquio de los enamorados?
El viento ha perdido
la dirección y la Madre Primavera muestra su pecho
cercenado.
Algo como un quebradero de huesos y de plumas
ha coronado de sombra los capitolios y llenado de cenizas
las casas que antes del fuego fueron blancas y púdicas como
    una guerra no declarada.
¡Aló aló Vietnam, aló padre y poeta Ho Chi Minh!
Hola, hermana ceniza, hermano dedo, hermanas barbas,
hola querido Comandante Guevara, viento-verdad, columna
    asesinada,
allá arriba de nosotros, cerca del cielo o del infierno,
algo ardiente como una roja espuma se levanta
—y es tu palabra insomne, tu agonía, la línea de tu sueño.

Pólvora y miedo en el país llamado
"el país más poderoso de la tierra".
En cada casa norteña, un becerro dorado.
En cada palacio del sur, la suma por centenares de esclavos.
En todas las casas una Biblia nunca leída, acaso murmurada,
    jamás entendida.

THIS IS CALLED THE BURNING FLAMES

Four horsemen with gunpowder waste the enormous gardens.
Four phantoms of lead dig a grave for love.
One, two, three, countless murderers
	behead the angel of happiness.
A horseman with bloodshot eyes rides among the flames.
Something like a distant sorrow occurs there,
in the country of grasslands, napalm,
	gold and enormous rivers
all of which suddenly rise up asking what's going on,
hello, hello, what's happening in the marble cities,
in the cities of miasma; what's happening that's broken
the love talk of lovers?
The wind has lost direction
and Mother Spring is pointing to her nipped-in-the-bud breasts.
Something like a fracturer of bones and feathers
has crowned the Capitols with darkness
and filled the houses with ashes which before the fire were white
and discreet like an undeclared war.
Hello, hello Vietnam, hello poet-priest Ho Chi Minh!
Hi there, sister ash, brother finger, sisters chins,
hi there, dear Commander Guevara, truth-wind,
	assassinated column,
up there above us all, close to the sky or close to hell
something hot like a red foam is rising—
and it's your tireless words, your agony, the outline of your dream.

Gunpowder and fear in the country called
"the most powerful country on earth."
In every house to the north, a golden calf.
In every mansion to the south, the end result
of hundreds of years of slavery.
In every household a Bible never read,
skimmed over perhaps yet never understood.

Pero olvidemos el poder, el orgullo, los becerros
y las Biblias—y no olvidemos a Abraham Lincoln río
    Mississippi abajo
casi al encuentro de don Benito Juárez desterrado
y liando tabaco virginiano; a Abraham Lincoln con su
    testimonio a cuestas,
su vigor de coloso y su tristeza secular.

Cuando Abraham Lincoln fue asesinado
un poco de atardecer cayó sobre el mundo de los negros
y las plegarias se sucedieron como un amargo río de lágrimas.
Llamearon las pupilas acusadoras, pero nada más. Ah, sí:
Un poeta de luenga barba blanca y ojos marinos se enfermó
    por la muerte de un capitán de la vida.
Los blancos habían empezado a linchar y
los capuchones del Ku Klux Klan erizaron el silencioso
    territorio.

Comenzaba a oler a pólvora, a sangre fresca,
a sudor de jinetes bramadores y a incendios.
Palomas delirantes aparecieron tal presagios,
hasta que los fusiles con miras telescópicas ocuparon
el lugar de los arcángeles y acallaron las aleluyas.
El agua del río padre tornóse espesa sangre
y el blues se arrinconó como un perro sarnoso.

Cuando hace pocos amaneceres asesinaron a
    Martin Luther King
un poco de niebla fustigó el mundo de los negros.
Pero entonces ya no solamente llamearon las pupilas
sino la madera, los minerales, los supermercados,
las farmacias, los bancos, las estaciones de policía,
las radiodifusoras, las estaciones de TV...
Ardieron de costa a costa las ciudades para que iluminaran
    una muerte

But let's forget the power, the pride, the calves
and the Bibles—and not forget
Abraham Lincoln, the Mississippi River down below him,
nearly meeting up with the exiled don Benito Juarez,
rolling Virginia tobacco; Abraham Lincoln
with his uphill testimony,
his colossal energy and his secular sadness.

When Abraham Lincoln was assassinated
a bit of dusk fell upon the Black world
and one after another the prayers followed
    like a bitter river of tears.
Accusing eyes blazed, but nothing more—
Oh, yes, a poet with a long white beard and sailor's eyes
was sickened by the death of a captain of life.
The whites had begun lynching
and the hooded ones of the Ku Klux Klan
stood the silent territory on end.
It began to smell of gunpowder, of fresh blood,
of the sweat of bellowing horsemen and of burning flames.
Delirious doves really seemed like omens,
up until guns with telescopic gazes
occupied the place of archangels
and silenced the hallelujahs.
The water in the almighty river turned into thick blood
and the blues were put in a corner like a mangy dog.

Since they assassinated Martin Luther King not long ago
a bit of confusion lashed the world of the Blacks.
But then not only have eyes gone up in flames
but wood, minerals, supermarkets,
pharmacies, banks, police stations,
radio stations, TV stations...
Cities have burned from coast to coast to illuminate a death

y hubiera un destello de esperanza en la piel negra y en la
   piel roja,
y hasta un poco de luz de algo que se llamó bondad, ¿o se
   llamaba piedad,
o bíblicamente, malditamente se llamaba violencia?
Hoy nada sabemos. Ni siquiera dónde empieza la cola de una
   serpiente de plomo
ni dónde termina el dolor de una viuda–ni qué entraña se
   arrancaron los huérfanos
para gemir muertos de angustia en las noches de Memphis y
   de Atlanta.

Se necesita ser muy hombre para no ser violento.
Se necesita saber musitar un versículo.
Hoy necesito
mucha cobardía para callarme la oración
por Martin Luther King,
y para no decir nada sobre la sangre que lo ahogó
como a un cordero para holocausto
en la piedra solar de una colina mosaica.

¡Aló aló Martin Luther King, hombre negro degollado!
Hola Martín Lutero Rey, pacífico hacedor de incendios,
campanada king king de la rebelión, tam tam descuartizado,
suave africano de la dura Norteamérica.

Aló asesinado
aló mortificado en cuerpo y alma
aló balaceado
Hola enterrado en alma y cuerpo
hola acribillado
santo negro de las llamas
de los negros incendios
te bendigo
te bendecimos
liberador.

which held a spark of hope for Black skin and Red skin,
including a quick flash of light
    from something called kindness,
or was it called mercy, or biblically and damningly
    called violence?
We're aware of nothing these days. Not even where the tail of
    a lead snake begins
or where the widow's pain ends;
    or how orphans started soul
in order to howl for those dead of anguish
    in the Memphis and Atlanta nights.

You have to really be a man not to be violent.
You have to know how to whisper a Bible verse.
Now I'd need
a lot of cowardice to silence me,
for a speech of Martin Luther King
to not say anything about the blood which choked him
like a lamb holocausted
on the solar stone of a mosaic hillside.

Greetings, greetings, Martin Luther King, Black man cut down
rousing king king of the rebellion, drum cut into pieces,
gentle African in callous North America.

Greetings assassinated one
mortified in body and soul
Hi targeted one
Hi buried in soul and body
Hi bullet-riddled one
Black saint of the flames
of Black conflagrations
I bless you
we bless you
liberator.

Ahora bendícenos, reverendo,
desde tu cielo ceñudo
desde la cálida oscuridad de tu celda celeste
¡No eres más que un cuchillo ni menos que un motín!
Por la muerte de Malcolm X
por la vida veloz de Stokely Carmichael
condúcenos, oh animoso,
                                        oh tumultuario
hacia el sofocante purgatorio
        de los vastos jardines incendiados!

9-10 de abril de 1968

Bless us now, Reverend,
from your scowling sky
from the warm darkness of your heavenly cell.
You're nothing more than a knife
or less than a riot;
Through the death of Malcolm X
and the swift life of Stokely Carmichael
lead us, oh spirited one, oh riotous one,
toward the suffocating purgatory
of enormous gardens in flames!

April 9-10, 1968

MATAR A UN POETA CUANDO DUERME

1

LE DISPARARON aquí mísmo, mire.
Mire y escuche mi sangre. En esta arteria,
de abajo arriba, para que la bala llegara al cerebro
y deshiciera bruscamente su genio y su infinito amor.

(Los chacales *erpianos* se habían dicho:
"Que sea cuando esté dormido.
Los pobres poetas son muy sensibles...")

Lo drogaron para matarlo
—porque para las bestias el mejor poeta
es un poeta muerto.

Mire cómo ese río se detuvo.
Oiga con cuidado la condenatoria palabra
del ceibo joven y el murmullo dolorido
de las maduras palmeras.

Dios de dioses, qué canallísimos fueron
y qué suciamente manejaron ese crimen.

2

Tan dulce, tan poeta, tan Roque,
tan mi Roquito Dalton.
Mira que te he llorado, camarada, muchas noches.
Óyeme que te he visto aquí, en México, y recordado
aquella noche de nuestro abrazo en el Tropicana;
las charlas en las afueras del Habana Libre;
en el Hotel Nacional y las discusiones
con el hermano Óscar Collazos;

THE MURDER OF A POET WHILE SLEEPING

1

Look, they shot him right here.
Look and listen to my blood. In this artery,
from the bottom up, so that the bullet entered his brain
and shattered his genius and infinite love.

(The harpy jackals had been saying:
"Let it happen while he's sleeping.
Poor poets are very sensitive...")

So they drugged him in order to murder him
—because for the beasts the greatest poet
is a dead poet.

I think about why that river stopped flowing.
It listens carefully to the condemned words
of the young and the painful rustling
of the ripe palm trees.

God of gods, what a gang they were
and how dirty the way they managed that crime.

2

So gentle one, so poet, so Roque,
so my dear little Roquito Dalton.
See, I've wept many nights for you, comrade.
Listen to me who's seen you here in Mexico,
and remembered that night of our embrace in the Tropicana;
the chats in the outskirts of Havana Libre;
and those discussions inside the National Hotel
with our brother Oscar Collazos;

la noche de diciembre de 1969 en que subiste
a mi habitación (la 544 del Nacional) a despedirte
para no vernos nunca más.
En una bolsa de papel llevabas un tesorito:
un limón gigante, dos naranjas, un jitomate
y el libro de poemas que me debías.

Pero esta noche de marzo,
a casi un año de que te asesinaron,
ya no tengo más libros tuyos
(sólo la Carta que te escribió Retamar
y el poema de Mario Benedetti);
no tengo ya sino unas cuantas lágrimas.

Esta noche nuestra, Roquito,
mi Roquito, siento que un poco
un poco de tu nobilísima sangre salvadora
me corre por alguna vena
en esta conspiración de la vida
por hacer más larga mi agonía.

Pienso ahora en Otto-René Castillo,
en Huberto Alvarado y en Javier Heraud,
poetas, combatientes, mutilados.

Hoy quiero vivir más,
no mucho, por tu sonrisa magnífica,
flaco queridísimo,
        totalmente vivo:
        Roque Dalton

that night in December 1969 when you came up
to my room (room 544 of the National Hotel)
to say goodbye, never to see each other again.
In a paper bag you were carrying a little treasury:
one gigantic lemon, two oranges, a tomato
and a book of poems you owed me.

But this night in March,
nearly a year after they assassinated you,
I don't have many books of yours
(only the letter that Retamar wrote for you
and a poem for Mario Benedetti);
I don't have anything now except these tears.

This night is ours, dear Roque,
my Roque, and I feel that a little
a little of your most noble Salvadorean blood
flows through some vein of mine
in this conspiracy for life
to make my agony even greater.

And now I'm thinking of Otto René Castillo,
of Huberto Alvarado and of Javier Heraud;
poets, guerrilla fighters, mutilated ones.

And now I want to live longer, not too much,
through your magnificent smile,
skinny, affectionate,
    totally alive:
    Roque Dalton.

PRESENCIA DE
FEDERICO GARCÍA LORCA

Dos voces suenan: el reloj y el viento,
mientras flota sin ti la madrugada.

1

Cuando todavía no nace el último lirio
y los ruidos quieren ya convertirse
en tibia y maravillosa alegría de las nubes,
y las mujeres sonríen blancamente acariciadas
por el dulce calor de nuestras manos,
y los niños son más flores que niños,
y las palabras como estrellas tristes,
y los barcos invernaderos.

Cuando el odio se resuelve en ceniza
porque los fusiles son realmente fusiles,
y la sangre verdadera y fresca sangre,
y una mano cercenada es como un pañuelo.

Cuando tu voz, Federico, noble voz
de helecho o niebla con jacintos naciendo.
Y de La Habana me llega tu grito aventurero,
del East River tu cínico desnudo al mar
y de Buenos Aires tus canciones como cuchillos.

Cuando desesperadamente te esperamos en México,
varón de tierra y cielo, dios de la espiga,
con tu sabroso cargamento de poemas y
guitarras de agua,
vestido de habitante de los ríos.

THE PRESENCE
OF FEDERICO GARCÍA LORCA

Two voices dream: the clock and the wind,
while the dawn drifts along without you.

1

Since the ultimate lily hasn't been born yet
and noises want to change themselves
into the warm marvelous joy of the clouds,
and women smile brightly caressable
by the gentle warmth of our hands,
and children are more flowers than children,
and words are like sad stars,
and ships docked for the winter.

When hatred resolves itself in ashes
because rifles are really rifles,
and real blood, fresh blood,
and a pared hand is like a handkerchief.

When your voice, Federico, your noble voice
made of ferns or clouds or blooming hyacinths.
Your adventurer's cry reaches me from Havana,
your naked cynicism of the sea from the East River
and from Buenos Aires your songs like knives.

Since we desperately await you in Mexico,
man of earth and sky, god of the ear of corn
with your distinctive bundle of poems
and guitars of water
dressed as a resident of rivers.

Cuando, por fin, tú mísmo estás de luz
en las albas y los atardeceres,
aparecen de pronto los crímenes y el llanto:
aparece tu Muerte, especial Muerte tuya,
hecha de pieles de gacelas y pólvora,
y suspiros amargos de terribles claveles;
hecha de melancolía exprimida
y mariposas, y música marina, y laureles,
y viento de palmeras, y sudor.

2

Federico: son las seis de la tarde
en la ciudad de Mérida; la Península nuestra
llora y se enluta por tu valiente sangre,
por tu sagrada sangre de mar, aurora y selva;
por tu estupenda sangre de saludable ángel
o demonio moreno: por tu madura sangre de gitano
y Hombre del Universo.

3

Tendría yo que apagar con el alma
todas las risas del mundo,
los ruidos turbios de la luna
y la falsa tristeza de las estrellas
por oírte pasar, Caballero de Plata y Azucenas,
encima de nosotros, tus partidarios de siempre,
dándonos la consigna necesaria
contra los negros perros que te rompieron
el corazón y la virtud de castigar a los maricas;
contra esos que te abrieron por mitad
y se acobardaron al encontrar
que eras lleno de rosas y gritos amarillos;

Since at last you are the light itself
in dawns and sunsets,
suddenly crimes and weeping appear;
your death appears, a special death just for you,
made of gazelle skins and gunpowder,
bitter moans of terrible carnations,
made of wrung-out melancholy and butterflies,
ocean music, laurels,
wind through palm trees, and sweat.

2

Federico: it's six in the afternoon
in the city of Mérida; this peninsula of ours
weeps and goes into mourning for your heroic blood,
for your sacred blood of the sea, dawn and jungle;
for your stupendous blood of an angel of mercy
or of a dark-skinned devil; for your ripe blood of a gypsy
and Universal Man.

3

I'll have to silence with my soul
all the laughter of the world,
the muddled noises of the moon
and the false sadness of the stars
hearing you pass by, Cavalier of Silver and White Lilies,
above all of us, your accustomed partisans
giving us the necessary password
against the black dogs who tore apart your heart
and your power to chastise the milksops;
against those who opened up to you halfway
and then chickened out upon finding
that you were full of roses and yellow cries;

contra esos bárbaros de cerebro de piedra
y maniobras de víboras cristianas:
contra esos que provocan a la URSS y asesinan
a Thaelmann y a Prestes lentamente;
contra esos verdugos de la Inteligencia humana,
tu consigna, tu consigna viril
de ave y bandera nuestra, Federico.

4

Verdad que hay una Muerte para piano
y otra para canarios; lo dijiste.
Verdad que hay cementerios y campanas,
que hay miseria y opresión en el mundo,
que hay automóviles y perlas rodando
por las avenidas del asco y el desprecio,
que hay millones de ojos mirándote a los ojos,
que hay las voces de Rafael Alberti y Pablo Neruda
para dar a los hombres la perfecta
sensación de tu vida continuada y magnífica
y eternamente guiando nuestros actos.

5

Estoy en un crepúsculo de la ciudad de Mérida
viéndote navegar gritando al mundo
la verdad de los crímenes de aquellos
que quisieran hacer trizas la estrella
que tuviste en la frente con tu Muerte:
estrella roja y pura como nube quemada,
estrella del presente y el futuro
con la que tú caminas, joven del infinito,
aliento superior de la España que sangra,
recio vino andaluz, rey jazmín de Granada,

against those brainy barbarians of stone
and the maneuvers of Christian vipers;
against those who provoke the USSR and who slowly
assassinated Thaelmann and Prestes;
against those butchers of human intelligence,
your password, your virile password
of wings and our flag, Federico.

4

It's true that there is a death for pianos
and another for canaries: you said that.
It's true that there are cemeteries and bells,
misery and oppression in the world,
automobiles and pearls roaming
along avenues of disgust and scorn,
that there are millions of eyes looking into other eyes,
that there are the voices of Rafael Alberti and Pablo Neruda
giving to men the perfect sensation
of your continuous and magnificent life
eternally guiding our actions.

5

I am in the twilight in the city of Mérida
visualizing you going around shouting at the world
the truth behind the crimes of those
who'd wanted to make shreds of the star
that you held opposite your Death:
a pure red star like a cloud on fire,
a star of the present time and of the future
with which you walk as a young man of the infinite
superior courage of bleeding Spain,
and strong Andalusian wine, jasmine king of Grenada,

hermano del crepúsculo que sufro sollozando,
nervios de golondrina, huesos de Tiempo,
maciza alma de niebla, Federico García.

16 de octubre de 1936

a brother of the twilight I suffer full of tears,
the nerves of a swallow, the bones of Time,
the massive soul of the mist, Federico Garcia.

October 16, 1936

ESA SANGRE

No la veo; no me baña su doloroso color,
ni la oigo correr sobre las piedras,
ni mis manos la tocan,
ni mis cabellos se oscurecen,
ni siquiera mis huesos se ponen amarillos,
ni aun mi saliva es verde, amarga y pálida.

No la he visto. No. No la he sentido
en mi propia sangre revolotear
como pájaro perdido, llorando
o nada más en busca de descanso.

Es horrible que no llueva sangre española
sobre las ciudades de América
como sangre de toros embistiendo
o lágrimas de águilas.

Pero sí, sí la veo, sí corre
por el cielo de mi ciudad,
sí la tocan mis manos,
sí mis cabellos oscurecen de miedo,
sí mi boca es una herida espantosa
y mis huesos roja pesadumbre.

La he visto, la he tocado
con mis propios asustadizos dedos,
y todavía estoy quejándome de pena,
de noche, de nostalgia.

Yo soy testigo de esa sangre.

THAT BLOOD

I don't see it; its sad color doesn't cover me,
I don't hear it run over the stones,
my hands don't touch it,
my hair doesn't hide from it,
my bones don't even wear yellow
nor is my spit green, bitter and pale.

I have not seen it. No. I have not felt it
flutter up in my own blood
like a lost bird, crying
or anything else in search of rest.

It's horrible that it does not rain Spanish blood
on the cities of America
like the blood of wounded bulls
or the tears of eagles.

But yes, yes, I see it, yes it runs
across the sky of my city,
yes my hands touch it,
yes my hair hides from fear,
yes my mouth is a terrible wound
and my bones red grief.

I have seen it, I have touched it
with my own frightened fingers,
and I am still moaning from the pain,
from night and nostalgia.

I am witness to that blood.

Puedo decir que hablé con ella
como un árbol ensangrentado
con una casa deshabitada;
puedo decir a los incrédulos
que en su corriente iban,
secos, mudos, ojos y ojos de jóvenes,
ojos y ojos de niños,
manos, manos de ancianos,
y vientres prodigiosos de muchachas,
y brazos prodigiosos de muchachos,
y mucho, muchísmo dolor,
y dientes españoles,
y sangre, siempre sangre.

Yo era. Yo era simplemente
antes de ver esa sangre.
Ahora soy, estoy, completo,
desamparado, ensordecido,
demasiado muerto para poder, después,
ver con serenidad ramos de rosas
y hablar de las orquídeas.

Yo soy testigo de esa sangre,
de esas palomas, de esos geranios,
de esos ojos con sal,
de aquellos mustios vientres
y sexos apagados.

Yo soy, testigo muerto, testigo de la sangre
derramada en España,
reverdecida en México
y viva en mi dolor.

I can say that I spoke with it
like a blood-stained tree
speaks to a vacant house;
I can say to those who doubt
that in its current flowed
the silent dry eyes upon eyes of the young,
eyes upon eyes of children,
hands, hands of the old,
and the beautiful bellies of young girls,
and the beautiful arms of young boys,
and much, much sorrow,
and Spanish teeth,
and blood, always blood.

I existed. I simply existed
before seeing that blood.
Now I am, I'm complete,
abandoned, deafened,
too dead to be able to later
look at rose branches with serenity
and speak of orchids.

I am witness to that blood,
to those doves, those geraniums,
those salty eyes,
those withered bellies
and extinguished sexes.

I am a dead witness, a witness to the blood
spilled in Spain
which sprouts again in Mexico
and lives in my pain.

ELLOS ESTÁN AQUÍ

Los cadáveres, las lágrimas, los quejidos,
la sombra de Madrid. Aquí están.
Esos lamentos grandes como árboles creciendo,
como nubes cubriendo las montañas.
Los ha traído el Atlántico.
Están sobre las rocas, sobre las playas amarillas,
sobre las llanuras torturantes, los ríos y los desiertos;
sobre las ciudades y las estaciones enmohecidas.
Es verdad todo eso: los gritos juveniles,
las dos últimos gotas de sangre del poeta,
el denso humo, el frío, la agitación,
la angustia de Sevilla, el estertor de Málaga.
El océano es violento, es maternal,
es misterioso y rudo,
es negro, azul y verde.
Pero es claro, y es rojo,
intensamente rojo cuando trae los ruidos
que nacen en España.

Y sobre largas playas y sobre recias rocas
el desaliento cae, rueda la pobre sangre,
mueren las lentas voces de quienes arrojaron
su desprecio, su heroica bofetada
a la traición, al crimen,
a los buitres de Italia y Alemania,
a los piratas del Mediterráneo,
a los uniformes pardos erizados de hachas,
a los curas o bestias que bendicen
el brusco asesinato de la tierra española.

Son como nubes esos tiernos lamentos,
como violetas de metal las lágrimas,
como angustioso río esa sangre,

160

HERE THEY ARE

The corpses, the tears, the moans,
the shadow of Madrid. Here they are.
These enormous moans like trees growing,
like clouds covering the mountains.
The Atlantic has brought them.
They're on the rocks, on the yellow beaches,
on the tortured prairies, the rivers and the deserts;
above the cities and the rusty stations.
All that is true: the youthful cries,
the final two drops of the poet's blood,
the thick smoke, the cold, the agitation,
the anguish of Seville, the death rattle of Málaga.
The ocean is violent, maternal,
mysterious and rough,
black, blue and green.
But it's clear, and it's red,
intensely red when it brings the sounds
that are born in Spain.

And upon the long beaches and upon the massive rocks
discouragement settles, the poor blood runs down,
the slow voices of those who hurled their scorn,
their heroic punch
at the treachery, at the crime,
at the vultures from Italy and Germany,
at the pirates of the Mediterranean,
at the drab bristly uniforms of the hatchetmen,
at the priests or the idiots who praise
the violent assassination of the Spanish earth.

Those soft moans are like clouds,
the tears like metallic violets,
that blood like an anguished river,

como secas consignas esas bocas abiertas,
esos ojos de hielo, esos puños de mármol.
Como enormes puñales esos tibios cadáveres.
Como tajantes dagas rasgando nuestro sueño,
las distancias, las olas del océano.

Aquí están. Pertenecen al aire,
al suelo, a los edificios, a las calles,
al agua, al entusiasmo o pena
que cada día vivímos.
Nos pertenecen estos muertos, esta gloria perfecta.
Ved a este miliciano: campesino,
veinte años, una herida en el vientre;
tiene ojos castellanos y mirada de fiebre.
Duerme su noble sombra con nosotros;
duerme su joven cuerpo bajo ruinas.
Ved a este niño: madrileño,
cinco anos, el cuerpo destrozado;
tiene sonrisa de ave, tiene ojos de miseria.
Yace su sombra débil en tierra mexicana;
su cuerpo, incinerado.

A los umbrales húmedos de nuestra Patria
llegan los hombres verdes a lamentos,
llegan los cuerpos rotos,
las mujeres sin senos,
los niños sin su fresca alegría,
los milicianos abatidos por los beduinos.
Llegan las venas, las vísceras, los huesos,
los músculos: el ejemplo sonoro
de los trabajadores españoles.

Y es triste, lastimoso, rabioso,
desesperante y feo el sentimiento.

Ved que han llegado ellos, camaradas.

those open mouths like dry instructions,
those icy eyes, those marble fists.
Those tepid corpses are like enormous daggers.
Our dream is like sharp daggers
slashing the distances, the ocean waves.

Here they are. They belong to the air,
to the ground, to the buildings, to the streets,
to the water, to the enthusiasm or suffering
we live each day.
These deaths, this perfect glory, belong to us.
Look at this militia: a twenty year old peasant
with a wound in the belly;
he has Castilian eyes and a feverish look.
His noble shade sleeps with us,
his young body sleeps under the ruins.
Look at this child from Madrid;
five years old, the body smashed;
it has a bird's smile, it has destitute eyes.
Its feeble shade lies in the Mexican earth,
its body burned.

At the damp thresholds of our native land
the unseasoned moaning men arrive,
and broken down bodies arrive,
and women without breasts,
and children without their fresh happiness,
and soldiers brought down by the barbarians.
Veins, guts, bones,
and muscles arrive: the blaring example
of the Spanish workers.

And the feeling is sad, pitiful, furious,
infuriating and ugly.

Comrades, look at how they've arrived.

DECLARACIÓN DE AMOR

1

Ciudad que llevas dentro
mi corazón, mi pena,
la desgracia verdosa
de los hombres del alba,
mil voces descompuestas
por el frío y el hambre.

Ciudad que lloras, mía,
maternal, dolorosa,
bella como camelia
y triste como lágrima,
mírame con tus ojos
de tezontle y granito,
caminar por tus calles
como sombra o neblina.

Soy el llanto invisible
de millares de hombres.
Soy la ronca miseria,
la gris melancolía,
el fastidio hecho carne.
Yo soy mi corazón
desamparado y negro.

Ciudad, invernadero,
gruta despedazada.

2

Bajo tu sombra, el viento del invierno
es una lluvia triste, y los hombres, amor,

DECLARATION OF LOVE

City that you carry within
my heart, my pain,
the greenish disgrace
of the men of dawn,
a thousand insolent voices
because of cold and hunger.

City which weeps for my city,
maternal, full of woe,
beautiful as a camellia
and sad as a tear,
look at me with your eyes
of volcanic stone and granite,
passing through your streets
like a shadow or like mist.

I am the invisible weeping
of thousands of men.
I am the roar of misery,
the grey sadness,
boredom made flesh.
I am my own derelict
black heart.

The city in winter,
a grotto torn to pieces.

Beneath your shadow, the winter wind
is a sad rain, and men, my love,

son cuerpos gemidores, olas
quebrándose a los pies de las mujeres
en un largo momento de abandono
–como nardos pudriéndose.
Es la hora del sueño, de los labios resecos,
de los cabellos lacios y el vivir sin remedio.

Pero si el viento norte una mañana,
una mañana larga, una selva,
me entregara el corazón deshecho
del alba verdadera, ¿imaginas, ciudad,
el dolor de las manos y el grito brusco, inmenso,
de una tierra sin vida?
Porque yo creo que el corazón del alba
es un millón de flores,
el correr de la sangre
o tu cuerpo, ciudad, sin huesos ni miseria.

Los hombres que te odian no comprenden
cómo eres pura, amplia,
rojiza, cariñosa, ciudad mía;
cómo te entregas, lenta,
a los niños que ríen,
a los hombres que aman claras hembras
de sonrisa despierta y fresco pensamiento,
a los pájaros que viven limpiamente
en tus jardines como axilas,
a los perros nocturnos
cuyos ladridos son mares de fiebre,
a los gatos, tigrillos por el día,
serpientes en la noche,
blandos peces al alba;
cómo te das, mujer de mil abrazos,
a nosotros, tus tímidos amantes:
cuando te desnudamos, se diría
que una cascada nace del silencio

are moaning bodies, waves
breaking at the feet of women
in a long moment of abandonment
like rotting spikenard.
It's the hour of dreaming, of parched lips,
of lank hair and life without a cure.

But if the north wind one morning,
one long jungle morning,
delivered the broken heart
of true dawn to me, can you imagine, city,
the painful hands and the huge sudden scream
from a lifeless earth?
Because I believe the heart of the dawn
is a million flowers,
the flow of blood
or your body city, without bones or misery.

The men who hate you don't understand
how pure, spacious,
reddish and loving you are, my city;
how you slowly surrender
to the children who laugh,
to the men who love bright women
with wide-awake smiles and clear thoughts,
to the birds who live cleanly
in your axial gardens,
to the nocturnal dogs
whose barks are feverish oceans,
to the cats, little jaguars during the day,
snakes at night,
sensual fish at dawn;
how you give yourself, woman of a thousand embraces,
to us, your timid lovers:
when we strip you naked, you'll tell yourself
a waterfall is being born in the silence

donde habitan la piel de los crepúsculos,
las tibias lágrimas de los relojes,
las monedas perdidas,
los días menos pensados
y las naranjas vírgenes.

Cuando llegas, rezumando delicia,
calles recién lavadas
y edificios-cristales,
pensamos en la recia tristeza del subsuelo,
en lo que tienen de agonía los lagos
y los ríos,
en los campos enfermos de amapolas,
en las montañas erizadas de espinas,
en esas playas largas
donde apenas la espuma
es un pobre animal inofensivo,
o en las costas de piedra
tan cínicas y bravas como leonas;
pensamos en el fondo del mar
y en sus bosques de helechos,
en la superficie del mar
con barcos casi locos,
en lo alto del mar
con pájaros idiotas.

Yo pienso en mi mujer:
en su sonrisa cuando duerme
y una luz misteriosa la protege,
en sus ojos curiosos cuando el día
es un mármol redondo.
Pienso en ella, ciudad,
y en el futuro nuestro:
en el hijo, en la espiga,
o menos, en el grano de trigo
que será también tuyo,

where the skin of the twilight,
the warm tears of clocks,
lost coins,
thoughtless days
and virgin oranges live.

When you arrive, oozing happiness,
at newly washed streets
and plate-glass buildings,
we'll be thinking about the sadness of the subsoil,
about the suffering
lakes and rivers go through,
and the sickly poppy fields,
and the mountains covered with thorns,
about those long beaches
where the surf
is a poor tame animal,
or about the shores of stone
brazen and forceful as lions;
we'll be thinking about the bottom of the sea
and about your fern forests,
about the surface of the sea
with ships nearly mad,
about the crest of the sea
with its idiotic birds.

I think about my woman:
about her smile when she sleeps
as a mysterious light shields her,
about her curious eyes when the day
is round marble.
I think about her, city,
and about our future:
about the child, about the ear of corn,
or even about the grain of wheat
that will also be yours,

porque es de tu sangre,
de tus rumores,
de tu ancho corazón de piedra y aire,
de nuestros fríos o tibios,
o quemantes y helados pensamientos,
humildades y orgullo, mi ciudad.

Mi gran ciudad de México:
el fondo de tu sexo es un criadero
de claras fortalezas,
tu invierno es un engaño
de alfileres y leche,
tus chimeneas enormes
dedos florando niebla,
tus jardines axilas la única verdad,
tus estaciones campos
de toros acerados,
tus calles cauces duros
para pies varoniles,
tus templos viejos frutos
alimento de ancianas,
tus horas como gritos
de monstruos invisibles,
¡tus rincones con llanto
son las marcas de odio y de saliva
carcomiendo tu pecho de dulzura!

because it's made of your blood,
of your murmuring,
of your big heart of stone and air,
of our cool or lukewarm
or burning or frozen thoughts,
humilities and pride, my city.

My great Mexico City:
the depth of your sex is a breeding ground
for bright strengths;
your winter is a lure
of pin money and milk;
your enormous smokestacks
fingers spewing fog;
your axial gardens the only truth;
your stations fields
of steely bulls;
your streets hard riverbeds
for vigorous feet;
your temples old fruit
food for old women;
your hours like screams
of invisible monsters;
your weeping corners
are the signs of hatred and spit
eating away your soft gentle heart!

EL VIEJO Y LA PÓLVORA

a Jesús Arellano

Viejo sangre de toro
viejo marino anciano de las nieves
viejo de guerras de enfermerías
de heridas
        Viejo con piel de flor
viejo santo de tanto amor
viejo de juventud niño de canas
viejo amadasantamente loco de amor siempre
viejo perro soldado
                anciano de los trópicos
viejo hasta lo eterno
joven hasta el espacio azul de muerte
Viejo viejo cazador
matador amador
amante amante amante amante
Puntual exactamente amante
lento y certero
marino viejo tempestad y bochorno
sudor de manos

        Viejo dios todos los días
de Dios escribir amar beber maldecir
beber tu propia sangre
viejo sangre de res
bendita seas maldita sangre tuya
cuando el disparo
seco bestial rotundo como un templo mancillado
degolló la marea la selva la cumbre las heridas

THE OLD ONE AND THE GUNPOWDER

for Jesús Arellano

Old blood of a bull
old sailor old man of the snows
old from the wars from the hospitals
from the wounds
                    Old with the skin of a flower
old saint with so much love
old from youth grey-haired child
old saintly lover crazy from love all the time
old soldier dog
                    grown old from the tropics
old until eternal
young until the blue space of death
Old old hunter
loving bullfighter
lover lover lover lover
Conscientious exacting lover
slow and sure
old sailor tempest and hot breeze
sweat of the hands

                    Old without malice every day
with god writing loving drinking cursing
drinking your own blood
the old blood of heads of cattle
blessed be that damned blood of yours
when the dry brutish shot
round as a stained temple
beheaded the tide the forest the summit the wounds

el amor total el infortunio la dicha la embriaguez
y un rostro dio fulgores amarillos a la muerte
y un ataúd de pólvora un ataúd un ataúd
y dos palabras
                  Ernest Hemingway

                                       5 de julio de 1966

a great love misfortune good luck drunkenness
and one face gave yellow brilliance to death
and a coffin of dust a coffin a coffin
and two words
                    Ernest Hemingway

                              July 5, 1966

SÍLABAS POR EL MAXILAR
DE FRANZ KAFKA

Oh vieja cosa dura, dura lanza, hueso impío, sombrío objeto
de árida y seca espuma; ola y nave, navío sin rumbo,
derrumbado
y secreto como la fórmula del alquimista; velero sin piloto
por un mar de aguda soledad; barca para pasar al otro
    lado del mundo,
enfilados hacia el cielo praguense y las callejuelas
donde la muerte pisa charcos de la cerveza que no bebió Neruda;
hueso infinito para ponerse verde de envidia,
para no remediar nada—ni el silencio ni las alas
oscuras y obscenas de tus orejas;
para no ver siquiera la herida de tu boca
ni el incendio de allá arriba, donde tus ojos todo lo penetran
como otras naves, otras lanzas ardidas, otra amenaza:
para hipnotizar la espada de la melancolía
y acaso para descifrar el curso de aquel río de palacios
donde murieron los santos y las vírgenes agonizaron
    tañendo laúdes de piedra;
para que pasen la novia y el féretro y Nezval resucite
en el corazón del follaje del cementerio judío;
para que el poeta te mire y se sonría ante el retrato de Dios;
para la locura—tu maxilar de duelo—,para la demencia total
y hasta para la humildad de nuestro lenguaje y su negra lucidez;
para morir eternamente de una tuberculosis dorada
y cabalgar las nubes y nombrar a los ángeles del exterminio
y clamar por los asesinos—otra vez allá arriba—,
por los que quemaron a Juan Huss
y arrojaron sus cenizas a un ancho río de espinosa corriente.
Hueso de piedra, ojo derecho del carlino puente,
pirámide caída, demolida, muerta desde su muerte;

SYLLABLES FOR THE JAWBONE
OF FRANZ KAFKA

Oh tough old thing, strong spear, irreligious bone,
somber object of hot dry foam; vessel and wave,
a lost ship secretly crumbling like the alchemist's plan;
a sailboat without a pilot in a sea of extreme solitude;
a boat for sailing to the other side of the world,
aimed at the Prague sky and the back alleys
where death steps into puddles of beer that Neruda never drank;
timeless bone which makes us green from envy
for which there is no remedy, neither for the silence
or the dark obscene wings of your ears;
the wound inside your mouth can't be seen
nor the passion above, where your eyes
penetrate everything like alien ships,
alien burning spears, alien threats to everything;
in order to hypnotize the sword of melancholy
and perhaps unravel the curse of that river of mansions
where saints die and suffering virgins pluck lutes made of stone
so that brides and coffins can pass
        and Nezval could come back to life
in the heart of the foliage in the Jewish cemetery;
so that the poet could watch and smile to himself
        before the image of God;
smile at madness—your jawbone of pain—
at total insanity and even at the humility of our language
        and its black clarity;
at dying eternally of a gilded tuberculosis
and at riding cloud-back and naming the exterminating angels
and screaming at the assassins—once more from up above—
at those who burned Jan Huss
and threw his ashes into a huge river of thorny currents.
Bone made of stone, upright eye of the sunken bridge,
demolished fallen pyramid, dead from its death;

hueso para escribir cien veces Señor K Señor K Señor K
hasta la podredumbre de las estrellas y las ratas de los castillos
y la infamia de los jueces; hueso vivo, puntiagudo
como la raíz del alma, como la ciega aurora de tus cejas;
hueso para llegar de rodillas y aguardar amorosamente
la carcajada y la oración, la blasfemia y el perdón.
Nave, navío, barca y espuma para sudar de miedo
y escribir sobre la piel la palabra abismo,
la palabra epitafio, la palabra sacrificio
y la palabra sufrimiento
                                y la palabra Hacedor.

a bone for writing Mr. K Mr. K Mr. K a hundred times
up to the decay of the stars and the rats
in the mansions and the infamy of judges;
a live bone, sharp as the root of the soul,
as the blind dawn of your eyebrows;
a bone for the arrival of knees and for fondly awaiting
laughter and prayers, blasphemy and pardon.
A vessel, a ship, a rowboat and foam for sweating with fear
and writing on the skin the word abyss,
the word epitaph, the word sacrifice
and the word suffering
                            and the word Maker.

CANCIÓN DE LA DONCELLA
DEL ALBA

Para Thelma

Se mete piel adentro
como paloma ciega,
como ciega paloma
cielo adentro.

Mar adentro en la sangre,
adentro de la piel.
Perfumada marea,
veneno y sangre.

Aguja de cristal
en la boca salada.
Marea de piel y sangre,
marea de sal.

Vaso de amarga miel:
sueño dorado,
sueño adentro
de la cegada piel.

Entra a paso despacio,
dormida danza;
entra debajo un ala,
danza despacio.

Domina mi silencio
la voz del alba.
Domíname, doncella,
con tu silencio.

SONG OF THE MAIDEN
OF THE DAWN

For Thelma

Skin intwined with skin
like dove blind,
like blind dove
heaven within.

Sea inside the blood,
within the skin.
Perfumed tide,
venom and blood.

Crystal needle
in the salty mouth.
Tide of skin and blood,
salt-tide.

Glass of bitter honey:
golden sleep,
dream inside
the blinded skin.

She enters in slow step,
sleep dancing;
she enters under a wing,
slowly the dance.

The voice of dawn
dominates my silence.
Dominate me, maiden,
with your silence.

Tómame de la mano,
llévame adentro
de tu callada espuma,
ola en la mano.

Silencio adentro sueño
con lentas pieles,
con labios tan heridos
como mi sueño.

Voy y vengo en la ola,
coral y ola,
canto canción de arena
sobre la ola.

Oh doncella de paz,
estatua de mi piel,
llévame de la mano
hacia tu paz.

Búscame piel adentro
anidado en tu axila,
búscame allí,
amor adentro.

Pues entras, fiel paloma,
pisando plumas
como desnuda nube,
nube o paloma.

Debo estar vivo, amor,
para saberte toda,
para beberte toda
en un vaso de amor.

Take me by the hand,
lead me inside
your silenced foam,
a wave in your hand.

Silence inside sleep
with sluggish skins,
with lips as wounded
as my dream.

I come and go with the wave,
coral and wave,
I sing a song of sand
over the wave.

Oh maiden of peace,
statue of my skin,
lead me by the hand
towards your peace.

Look for skin within,
beneath your arm,
look for me there,
with love inside.

Then you enter, loyal dove,
covering feathers slightly
like a naked cloud,
a cloud or a dove.

I need to be alive, love,
to know you completely,
to drink you completely
in a glass of love.

Alerta estoy, doncella
del alba; alerta
al sonoro cristal
de tu origen, doncella.

I'm aware, maiden
of the dawn; aware of
the resonant crystal
of your origin, maiden.

LOS RUIDOS DEL ALBA

I

Te repitito que descubrí el silencio
aquella lenta tarde de tu nombre mordido,
carbonizado y vivo
en la gran llama de oro de tus diecinueve años.
Mi amor se desligó de las auroras
para entregarse todo a tu murmullo,
a tu cristal murmullo de madera blanca incendiada.

Es una herida de alfiler sobre los labios tu recuerdo,
y hoy escribí leyendas de tu vida
sobre la superficie tierna de una manzana.

Y mientras todo eso,
mis impulsos permanecen inquietos,
esperando que se abra una ventana para seguirte
o estrellarse en el cemento doloroso de las banquetas.
Pero de las montañas viene un ruido tan frío
que recordar es muerte y es agonía el sueño.

Y el silencio se aparta, temeroso
del cielo sin estrellas,
de la prisa de nuestras bocas
y de las camelias y claveles desfallecidos.

II

Expliquemos al viento nuestros besos.
Piensa que el alba nos entiende:
ella sabe lo bien que saboreamos
el rumor a limones de sus ojos,
el agua blanca de sus brazos.

THE CLAMOR OF DAWN

I

I'll tell you once again I discovered silence
on that slow afternoon of your rotting name
reduced to ashes and alive
in the great golden flame of your nineteen years.
My love untied itself from the dawns
to surrender totally to your whispers,
your crystal whispers of charred white wood.

Your memory is a puncture wound on your lips,
and today I wrote legends of your life
on the tender surface of an apple.

And during all that,
my feelings remained on edge,
hoping a window would open in order to follow you
or to crash down on the painful cement sidewalk.
But from the mountains comes a noise so cold
to remember is death and to dream is agony.

And silence moves away,
fearful of the starless sky,
and of the urgency of our mouths
and of wilted camellias and faint carnations.

II

We explain our kisses to the wind.
Dawn thinks it understands us:
it knows it's good that we savor
the murmur of lemons in its eyes,
the white water in its arms.

(Parece que los dientes rasgan trozos de nieve.
El frío es grande y siempre adolescente.
El frío, el frío: ausencia sin olvido.)

Cantemos a las flores cerradas,
a las mujeres sin senos
y a los niños que no miran la luna.
Cantemos sin mirarnos.

Mienten aquellos pájaros y esas cornisas.
Nosotros no nos amamos ya.
Realmente nunca nos amamos.
Llegamos con el deseo y seguimos con él.
Estamos en el ruido del alba,
en el umbral de la sabiduría,
en el seno de la locura.

Dos columnas en el atrio
donde mendigan las pasiones.
Perduramos, gozamos simplemente.

Expliquemos al viento nuestros besos
y el amargo sentido de lo que cantamos.

No es el amor de fuego ni de mármol.

El amor es la piedad que nos tenemos.

(It seems like its teeth are ripping chunks of snow to pieces.
The cold is enormous and forever young.
The cold, the cold: absence without oblivion.)

We sing to hidden flowers,
to women without breasts
and to children who don't look at the moon.
We sing without looking at each other.

Those birds and those cornices are lying.
We don't love each other now.
In reality we never loved each other.
We arrive with desire and we arise with it.
We're inside the clamor of dawn,
at the threshold of wisdom,
at the breast of madness.

Two columns at the entrance
where passions go begging.
We endure, we enjoy ourselves simply.

We explain our kisses to the wind
and that bitter feeling we sing about.

It's not a love of fire or marble.

Love is the mercy we possess.

ELEGÍA DE LA ROSA BLANCA

Fuiste cuando el silencio era una voz de llovizna,
cuando sabias corolas daban el equilibrio al corazón de junio
y claras lunas tibias como pequeñas ruedas
llevaron al abismo los insomnios por turbios
y los deseos por vivos y angustiados.
Indelicada rosa blanca.
Desesperada rosa tierna.
Dueña del infinito y precursora de la contemplación y el tedio.
Rosa blanca: viviste puramente,
como apasionada y cansada frialdad,
como alba derrotista.
Eras como un dolor inmóvil
pero ceñido de ansias.
Te guardaba en mis manos creyéndote un silencio de nieve.
Eras torre y sirena.
Eras madera blanca o brisa.
Eras estrella distraída.
En las noches parecías una selva despierta,
muy mojada. Y al día
siguiente eras perla gigante
o tremenda montaña
o cristalina y rauda flor del tiempo.
Yo te seguía con furia y esperanza.

Vivo dueño de nada con tu muerte.

Vivo como una astilla de tristeza.

ELEGY FOR A WHITE ROSE

You existed when silence had a drizzly voice,
when wise corollas gave the heart of June balance
and clear tepid moons like little wheels
carried confused sleeplessness
and painful living desires into the abyss.
Tough white rose.
Tender frenzied rose.
Owner of infinity, forerunner of meditation and tedium.
White rose, you lived purely,
like a passionate and weary coolness,
like a defeatist dawn.
You were a motionless sorrow
yet encircled by worries.
I cupped you in my hands, believing you were a snowy silence.
You were tower and siren.
You were white wood or breeze.
You were a dreamy star.
At night you seemed to be a wide-awake
very wet jungle.
And the following day you were
a gigantic pearl or an awesome mountain
or a transparent impetuous flower of time.
I pursued you with fury and hope.

I live on, owner of nothing with your death.

I live like a splinter of sadness.

ALBA DESDE UNA ESTRELLA

Desde un cielo de nardos,
desde la roja soledad,
desde mi lenta vida solitaria
te contemplo, existente,
beso largo, manos con fiebre,
cabellos como luz submarina.
Desde una estrella mi deseo perfecto
y el alba fría de siempre y esperanza.

Oh rosa solitaria, pareces
un abismo y mil cadáveres de hielo,
contemplación, idea,
palabra pronunciada sin odio,
grito que por las calles
como liebre corriera;
pareces la sublevación de la tierra,
cuando los árboles y los ríos tiemblan
de incontenido rencor;
pareces, alba y rosa,
rebeldía que se enciende,
que se extiende como una verdad
en busca de los limpios horizontes:
las más altas montañas
o la más prodigiosa de las locuras.

Eres, en la intención, lejana
y construida pureza,
selva que avanza libre y soberana,
avalancha de nubes,
invasión de aves,
tormenta subterránea,
alegría sin descanso.

DAWN FROM A STAR

From a sky of nard,
from the red solitude,
from my slow, lonely life
I contemplate you existing,
a lengthy kiss, feverish hands,
hair like underwater light.
From a star my perfect desire
and cool customary dawn and hope.

Oh solitary rose, you're like
a canyon and a thousand frozen corpses,
a thought, an idea,
a word spoken without hatred,
a scream which carouses in the streets
like a rabbit;
you're the revolt of the earth,
when trees and rivers tremble
with uncontrollable anger;
dawn and rose, you're like
a revolution which catches fire,
spreading like truth
in search of pure horizons:
the highest mountains
or the greatest insanities.

In the plan you're distant
and built with purity,
a jungle which advances
free and sovereign,
an avalanche of clouds,
an invasion of birds,
an underground storm,
joy without rest.

Te amo desde una estrella,
te amo desde la poesía,
rosa sin cascabeles, sin suspiros,
sin traiciones. Te amo
como al otoño quejumbroso y viril,
como a los niños rubios
que inventan la pereza.

Existes. Te contemplo.

I love you from a star,
I love you from poetry,
breathless rose without bells,
without betrayals. I love you
like the vibrant plaintive autumn,
like blond children who invent laziness.

You exist. I think of you.

BORRADOR
PARA UN TESTAMENTO

A Octatvio Paz

1

Así pues, tengo la piel dolorosamente ardida de medio siglo,
el pelo negro y la tristeza más amarga que nunca.
No soy una lágrima viva y no descanso y bebo lo mismo
que durante el imperio de la Plaza Garibaldi
y el rigor en los tatuajes y la tuberculosis de la muchacha ebria.
Había un mundo para caerse muerto y sin tener con qué,
había una soledad en cada esquina, en cada beso;
teníamos un secreto y la juventud nos parecía algo
    dulcemente ruin;
callábamos o cantábamos himnos de míseria.
Teníamos pues la negra plata de los veinte años.
Nos dividíamos en ebrios y sobrios,
inteligentes e idiotas, ebrios e inteligentes, sobrios e idiotas.
Nos juntaba una luz, algo semejante a la comunión, y
una pobreza que nuestros padres no inventaron
nos crecía tan alta como una torre de blasfemias.

Las piedras nos calaban. No nos calentaba el sol.
Una espiga nos parecía un templo
y en un poema cabía el universo del amor.
Dije "el amor" como quien nada dice o nada oye.
Dije amor a la alondra y a la gacela,
a la estatua o camelia que abría las alas
y llenaba la noche de dulce espuma.
He dicho siempre amor como quien todo

196

SKETCH FOR A LAST WILL
AND TESTAMENT

for Octavio Paz

1

Well then, for half a century I've had the painfully burned skin,
my black hair and sadness more bitter than ever.
I'm not a living tear and I never rest and I drink
the same as during the empire of Garibaldi Market
and the harshness of the tattoos and the tuberculosis
    of the drunken girl.
I had a world that was penniless,
I had solitude in every corner, in every kiss;
we had a secret and youth seemed to us
    something sweetly cynical;
we were silent or we sang hymns about misery.
We were twenty years of black money old.
We seperated ourselves into drunks and sober ones,
intelligent ones and idiots, drunks and intelligent ones,
    sober ones and idiots.
We gathered together a light, something like communion,
and a poverty which our fathers didn't invent;
we grew as tall as a tower of insults.

The stones were sizing us up. The sun wasn't warming us up.
A spike looked like a temple to us
and the universe of love fit itself into the poem.
I said "love" like one who says nothing or hears nothing.
I said love to the skylark and the gazelle,
to the statue or the camellia that opened its wings
and filled the night with fresh mist.
I've always spoken of love like everyone

lo ha dicho y escuchado. Amor como azucena.
Todo brillaba entonces, como el alma del alba.

¡Oh juventud, espada de dos filos! ¡Juventud
medianoche, juventud mediodía,
ardida juventud de especie diamantina!

2

Teníamos más de veinte años y menos de cien
y nos dividíamos en vivos y suicidas.
Nos desangraba el cuchillo-cristal de los vinos baratos.
Así pues, flameaban las banderas como ruinas.
Las estrellas tenían el espesor de la muerte.
Bebíamos el amor en negras tazas de ceniza.
¡Ay ese amor, ese olor, ese dolor!
Esa dolencia en pleno rostro, aquella fatiga
de todos los días, todas las noches.

Eramos como estrellas iracundas:
llenos de libros, manifiestos, amores desolados,
desoladamente tristes *a la orilla del mundo,*
víctimas victoriosas de un
severo y dulce látigo de aura crepuscular.
Descubríamos pedernales-palabras,
dolientes, adormecidos ojos de jade
y llorábamos con alaridos de miedo
por lo que vendría después
cuando nuestra piel no fuera nuestra
sino del poema hecho y maltrecho,
del papel arrugado y su llama
de intensas livideces.

who has spoken about it and has listened. Love like a tiger lily.
Everything was shining then, like the soul of dawn.

Oh youth! Double-edged sword!
Midnight youth, high-noon youth,
angry youth of an adamant sort!

2

We had more than twenty years and less than a hundred
and we were divided into the live ones and the suicides.
The crystal knife of cheap wines made us bleed.
And then flags flared up like ruins.
Stars had the density of death.
We drank love from dark cupfuls of ashes.
Oh that love, that smell, that pain!
That aching full in the face, that weariness
all day and night long.

We were like raging stars:
filled with books, manifestos, abandoned loves,
grievously sad at the edge of the world,
victorious victims in a bittersweet
twilight breeze.
We invented words of flint,
sorrows, and drowsy jade eyes
and we wept with eyes of fear
for what would come afterward
when our skin was no longer ours
except in the poem created and abused
on crumpled paper and in its flame
of furious intensity.

3

Después,
dimos venas y arterias,
lo que se dice anhelos,
a redimir el mundo cada tibia mañana;
vivimos
una lluvia helada de bondad.
Todo alado, musical, todo guitarras
y declaraciones, murmullos del alba,
vahos y estatuas, trajes raídos, desventuras.
Estaban todos—y todos construían su poesía.
Diría sus nombres si algunos de ellos
no hubiesen vuelto ya a la dorada tierra,
adorados, añorados cada minuto
—el minutero es de piedra, sol y soledad—;
entonces, no es a los vivos sino a mis muertos
a quienes doy mi adiós, mi para siempre.

     A ellos y por ellos
y por la piedad que profeso
por el amor que me mata
por la poesía como arena
y los versos, los malditos versos
que nunca pude terminar,
dejo tranquilamente
                de escribir
                de maldecir
                de orar
                llorar
                amar.

3

Afterwards,
we gave veins and arteries,
what's meant by desire,
to redeem the world from every lukewarm tomorrow;
we lived
in a hail of kindness.
Everything, all guitars
and declarations, whispers at dawn,
vapors and statues, worn-out suits and misfortunes
were winged and musical.
Everyone existed and everyone was putting out their poetry.
I'd give their names if some of them
had not already returned to the golden earth,
adored, yearned for every minute
—the minute hand is made of stone, sun, and solitude—;
and so it's not to the living but to the dead
I deliver my farewell, my eternity.

      To them and for them
and for the mercy which I profess
for the love that kills me
for the poetry like sand
and the stanzas, the damned stanzas
I was never able to finish,
peacefully I stop
            writing
            cursing
            praying
            weeping
            loving.

ABOUT THE AUTHOR

Efraín Huerta was born in Silao, Guanajuato, Mexico on June 18, 1914, and died in Mexico City in 1982. Author of fifteen books of poetry, he was a professional journalist, specializing in film criticism, as well as a poet. During his lifetime he received numerous honors and awards, including the Palmas Academicas in France in 1945, the Villaurrutia Poetry prize in 1975, and the National Journalism Prize in 1978.

Huerta was part of the generation of the *Taller (Workshop)* literary movement, and with Octavio Paz produced the important literary magazine *Taller Poético* between 1938 and 1941. During much of his life, Huerta associated with the Mexican political artist José Clemente Orozco, and he met El Salvador's Roque Dalton in Mexico City in 1969. Huerta was always in the forefront of his generation as the one poet who constantly rallied for sweeping political and social change via his avowed faith in Marxism. He was also fascinated with the U. S. political scene and traveled widely in the United States from 1949 to 1953.

In verses that fuse highly original imagery with exuberant rhythms, Efraín Huerta probed the cultures of both Mexico and "el Norte," from the impact of racism in Mississippi to political corruption in Mexico. Since he demanded for life and art the same freedom he demanded for politics, his poetry is often erotic. His poems are passionate outcries to love and justice, characterized by original metaphors and an acerbic wit that earned him the nickname "Crocodile." Huerta empathized with victims worldwide, and in *500,000 Azaleas*, one finds homages to Che Guevara, Roque Dalton, Paul Robeson and Martin Luther King. His poetry is essentially humanistic, infused with a desire for liberty, dignity, and equality, though he always casts a cold, critical eye upon the world and lets his heart speak of the pain caused by the gap between dream and reality.

ABOUT THE CONTRIBUTORS

JACK HIRSCHMAN was born in New York City in 1933 and has lived since 1973 in San Francisco. He has written 74 chapbooks of poetry and has translated over 30 books in over eight languages. Since leaving a university teaching career in the 60s, Hirschman has taken the free exchange of poetry and politics into the streets where he has mentored a number of poets. He currently assists in the editing of *Left Curve* and is a correspondent for *The People's Tribune*. Among his many volumes of poetry are *A Correspondence of Americans* (Indiana U. Press, 1960), *Black Alephs* (Trigram Press, 1969), *Lyripol* (City Lights, 1976), *The Bottom Line* (Curbstone, 1988), and *Endless Threshold* (Curbstone, 1992).

JIM NORMINGTON has been translating the work of Latin American poets for over ten years. His last published book of translations is the *Selected Poems of Alfonsina Storni,* published in 1988 by White Pine Press. He has translated the work of Mexico's Alvaro Mutis and Guatemala's Flavio Herrera. A poet himself, his latest published book is *Book of Blues.* He is the recipient of the Year 2000 Wilkerson Fellowship from the Sacramento Metropolitan Arts Commission. He currently teaches English at Fremont Adult School in Sacramento, California.

ILAN STAVANS, a novelist and critic, teaches at Amherst College. His books include *The Hispanic Condition* (HarperCollins), *Art and Anger: Essays on Politics and the Imagination* (New Mexico), and *The Oxford Book of Latin American Essays.* He has been a National Book Critics Circle Award nominee and the recipient of the Latino Literature Prize.

CURBSTONE PRESS, INC.

is a non-profit publishing house dedicated to literature that reflects a commitment to social change, with an emphasis on contemporary writing from Latino, Latin American and Vietnamese cultures. Curbstone presents writers who give voice to the unheard in a language that goes beyond denunciation to celebrate, honor and teach. Curbstone builds bridges between its writers and the public – from inner-city to rural areas, colleges to community centers, children to adults. Curbstone seeks out the highest aesthetic expression of the dedication to human rights and intercultural understanding: poetry, testimonies, novels, stories, and children's books.

This mission requires more than just producing books. It requires ensuring that as many people as possible learn about these books and read them. To achieve this, a large portion of Curbstone's schedule is dedicated to arranging tours and programs for its authors, working with public school and university teachers to enrich curricula, reaching out to underserved audiences by donating books and conducting readings and community programs, and promoting discussion in the media. It is only through these combined efforts that literature can truly make a difference.

Curbstone Press, like all non-profit presses, depends on the support of individuals, foundations, and government agencies to bring you, the reader, works of literary merit and social significance which might not find a place in profit-driven publishing channels, and to bring the authors and their books into communities across the country. Our sincere thanks to the many individuals, foundations, and government agencies who support this endeavor: Connecticut Commission on the Arts, Connecticut Humanities Council, Daphne Seybolt Culpeper Foundation, Fisher Foundation, Hartford Courant Foundation, J. M. Kaplan Fund, Eric Mathieu King Fund, John D. and Catherine T. MacArthur Foundation, National Endowment for the Arts, Open Society Institute, Puffin Foundation, and the Woodrow Wilson National Fellowship Foundation.

Please help to support Curbstone's efforts to present the diverse voices and views that make our culture richer. Tax-deductible donations can be made by check or credit card to:
Curbstone Press, 321 Jackson Street, Willimantic, CT 06226
phone: (860) 423-5110   fax: (860) 423-9242
www.curbstone.org

IF YOU WOULD LIKE TO BE A MAJOR SPONSOR OF A
CURBSTONE BOOK, PLEASE CONTACT US.